Dryden's Heroic Drama

Dryden's Heroic Drama

By

ARTHUR C. KIRSCH

GORDIAN PRESS
NEW YORK
1972

Originally Published 1965
Reprinted 1972

Library of Congress Catalog Card Number—70-150412
ISBN—87752-136-0

ACKNOWLEDGMENTS

PORTIONS of Chapters I and IV first appeared in my article, "The Significance of Dryden's *Aureng-Zebe*," *ELH*, XXIX (1962), copyright 1962, by the Johns Hopkins Press, and a portion of Chapter II is based upon my essay, "Dryden, Corneille, and the Heroic Play," *MP*, LIX (1962), copyright 1962 by the University of Chicago Press. I wish to thank the editors of both periodicals for their courtesy in allowing me to reprint this material.

My research on this book was aided by generous grants from the Samuel S. Fels Fund and the Princeton University Research Fund, and by exceptionally considerate service at the British Museum, the Bodleian, the Folger, and the rare book rooms of the libraries of Princeton and Yale. I can mention here only a few of the many people who have helped me. Miss Miriam Brokaw and Professors Lawrence I. Lipking, Eric Rothstein and James Thorpe gave me valuable criticism. I also wish to thank Jack S. Goodfellow, my undergraduate assistant, who helped me check references and quotations, Mrs. Helen Wright, who typed the final manuscript, and Mrs. Marjorie Putney, who edited it for the Princeton University Press. I owe most to Professors Gerald E. Bentley and Alan S. Downer, who offered encouragement and criticism, first as thesis advisers and then as colleagues.

ARTHUR C. KIRSCH

Princeton, New Jersey

CONTENTS

Dryden's Heroic Drama

CHAPTER I

Dryden's Theory of the Rhymed Heroic Play

(i) Some provisos for reading Dryden's criticism

RYDEN'S criticism of heroic drama is extensive, but also easy to misread. For a long time
under contract to produce three plays a year
for the King's Company,[1] he was saturated in theatrical
affairs when he wrote the bulk of his dramatic criticism,
and most of his essays are designed primarily to support
and explore his practice. The immediate consequence of
this practical bias is that much of his criticism is occupied
with self-justification and even self-advertisement. He
was concerned about his literary reputation and always
found something to praise in his plays, heralding many
of them, when they were first published, as the best he
had yet written.[2] His claims for the rhymed heroic play

---

[1] See James M. Osborn, *John Dryden: Some Biographical Facts
and Problems* (1939), pp. 184-91.

[2] See especially dedication of *The Indian Emperour* (1667); preface to *Secret-Love* (1668); preface to *The Conquest of Granada*
(1672); dedication of *Aureng-Zebe* (1676); preface to *All for Love*
(1678); and dedication of *The Spanish Fryar* (1681). Dryden's
"puffs" were notorious in his own day. One critic of *Albion and
Albanius* (1685), for example, noted:

> With thy dull prefaces still thou wouldst treat us,
>   Striving to make thy dull bauble look fair;
> So the horned herd of the city do cheat us,
>   Still most commending the worst of their ware.

(Quoted in *The Works of John Dryden*, ed. Sir Walter Scott, rev.
and corr. by George Saintsbury, 18 vols. [Edinburgh, 1882-92], VII,
226.) There were many similar criticisms, especially of Dryden's

are especially marked by the tone, in his own words, of a gambler who has *"already swept the stakes."* Dryden labored under the shadow of his great Elizabethan predecessors—he once confessed that "There is no bayes to be expected in their Walks"[3]—and for a while, with the rhymed heroic play, he thought he had equalled and even surpassed them in certain respects. His enthusiasm, therefore, is understandable. But it is not necessarily informative. In writing about the heroic play he was inclined to emphasize his innovations and minimize his debts; and thus, to understand his plays with the help of his criticism we must make a distinction between what he said he was doing and what he in fact was doing.

We must also recognize that as a result of his orientation towards his own practice his criticism is not normally directed at theoretical issues. His concerns are usually concrete: characterization, language, stage effects, the relationship between dramatic conventions and the demonstrated taste of Restoration spectators. Even *Of Dramatick Poesie*, which purports to treat broader issues, resolves itself into a consideration of the theatrical traditions and conventions which are capable of pleasing a

---

alleged habit of recommending his own works by disparaging those of his predecessors: see, *e.g.*, *The Rehearsal* (1672), II, i, p. 13; [Richard Leigh], *The Censure of the Rota* (Oxford, 1673), p. 13; *The Friendly Vindication of Mr. Dryden* (Cambridge, 1673), pp. 11-12; Elkanah Settle, dedication of *The Empress of Morocco* (1673), sig. A2v; and [Thomas Brown], *The Reasons of Mr. Bays Changing his Religion* (1688), p. 15. All references to seventeenth-century texts are to first editions and place of publication is London, unless otherwise noted.

[3] *Of Dramatick Poesie* (1668), p. 65; XV, 367. The texts of the quotations from Dryden are always those of the first edition, but reference is also made to the Scott-Saintsbury edition of his works. Thus the reference, "p. 65; XV, 367," means that the text of the quotation is on page 65 of the first edition of *Of Dramatick Poesie* and may also be consulted in volume XV, page 367 of the Scott-Saintsbury edition.

contemporary English audience;[4] and the preface to *Troilus and Cressida*, his most ambitious exploration of the theoretical grounds of serious drama, is written fundamentally "*to enquire how far we ought to imitate our own Poets*, Shakespear *and* Fletcher *in their Trage- dies. . . .*" (sig. av; VI, 259)[5] Always empirical, Dryden also never hesitated to alter a critical position to conform to new directions in his plays. After a decade spent in defending rhymed verse for serious drama, he wrote in the preface to *All for Love* (1678): "In my Stile I have profess'd to imitate the Divine *Shakespeare*; which that I might perform more freely, I have dis-incumber'd my self from Rhyme. Not that I condemn my former way, but that this is more proper to my present purpose." (sig. b4v; V, 339) Such a comment is neither weak- minded nor inconsistent, as we shall see when we examine the reasons for Dryden's change, but nevertheless it does indicate Dryden's inclination to subordinate theoretical commitments to his practice.

Our understanding of these theoretical commitments, moreover, is further complicated by the limitations of the critical language which Dryden could employ to describe them. He did not have a strong analytical in- telligence; he constantly deferred to contemporary critics for analytical discriminations. He once remarked that "the *French* are as much better Criticks than the *English*, as they are worse Poets,"[6] a characteristically two-handed compliment which is nevertheless confirmed by his borrowings from a succession of French critics, including Corneille, Rapin, Dacier, Le Bossu, and

---

[4] For an illuminating discussion of the pragmatic character of *Of Dramatick Poesie* see David Daiches, *Critical Approaches to Literature* (Englewood Cliffs, N.J., 1956), pp. 174-76.

[5] See Hoyt Trowbridge, "Dryden's Essay on the Dramatic Poetry of the Last Age," *PQ*, XXII (1943), 240-50.

[6] Dedication of the *Aeneis* in *The Works of Virgil* (1697), sig. [b3]; XIV, 162.

[5]

Segrais. His deference to Rymer, in his own country, amounted almost to fear. Judging by the so-called "Heads of an Answer to Rymer," notations which he made in the end-papers of his copy of *The Tragedies of the Last Age* (1677), Dryden disagreed with Rymer on nearly every important issue, but he did not venture to answer him directly until Rymer had discredited himself with the absurdities of *A Short View* (1692). The preface to *Troilus and Cressida* (1679), which constitutes Dryden's earlier attempt to respond to Rymer's argument, is both hesitant and evasive.[7]

Dryden's difficulties with Rymer, however, are revealing because they are not simply the result of Dryden's lack of analytical skill. The "Heads of an Answer" shows quite clearly that Dryden knew where he differed from Rymer; his problem was in translating his disagreement into an effective criticism of Rymer's whole critical position. The cause of this problem seems to have been largely semantic. Late in his life Dryden remarked that when he began to write *Of Dramatick Poesie* (1668) he had few critical precedents to follow: "I was Drawing the Out-lines of an Art without any Living Master to Instruct me in it; an Art which had been better Prais'd than Study'd here in *England*, wherein *Shakespear* who Created the Stage among us, had rather Written happily, than knowingly and justly; and *Johnson* [sic], who by studying *Horace*, had been acquainted with the Rules, yet seem'd to envy to Posterity that Knowledge, and like an Inventor of some

---

[7] Dryden's first direct criticism of Rymer in print occurs in the dedication of *Love Triumphant* (1694). See also the letter to Dennis (1693), *The Letters of John Dryden*, ed. C. E. Ward (Durham, 1942), pp. 71-72. For a discussion of Dryden's less direct response to Rymer in the preface to *Troilus and Cressida*, see Fred G. Walcott, "John Dryden's Answer to Thomas Rymer's *The Tragedies of the Last Age*," *PQ* xv (1936), 194-214. See also George Watson, "Dryden's First Answer to Rymer," *RES*, N.S., xiv (1963), 17-23.

useful Art, to make a Monopoly of his Learning: . . . thus, as I may say, before the Use of the Loadstone, or knowledge of the Compass, I was sailing in a vast Ocean, without other help, than the Pole-Star of the Ancients, and the Rules of the *French* Stage amongst the Moderns, which are extreamly different from ours, by reason of their opposite taste. . . ."[8] Dryden exaggerates his difficulties. Jonson left a far more significant, if disconnected, body of criticism than Dryden here gives him credit for, and in *Of Dramatick Poesie* itself Dryden had been more generous, remarking that "in the precepts which [Jonson] has laid down in his Discoveries, we have as many and profitable Rules for perfecting the Stage as any wherewith the French can furnish us." (p. 50; XV, 348) Moreover, "A Defence of an Essay of Dramatique Poesie" shows that Dryden had consistent and coherent critical premises to work from.[9] Nevertheless his complaints about the primitive state of dramatic criticism in England have some justification and should be taken seriously. After Jonson there had been no concerted critical essays on the drama in England. Dryden therefore often did have to create a new vocabulary capable of justifying the nature and aims of contemporary plays; and in doing so he could not always anticipate the implications of the terms and premises he employed. The basic reason, in fact, that Rymer alarmed him was that Rymer could apparently use the same critical assumptions and language to arrive at opposite conclusions, conclusions which threatened the traditions which Dryden, as a practicing dramatist, was committed to defend; and Rymer's argument often showed that Dryden had not always thought through

[8] Dedication of *The Satires of Decimus Junius Juvenalis* (1693), p. ii; XIII, 3.

[9] See Hoyt Trowbridge, "The Place of Rules in Dryden's Criticism," *MP*, XLIV (1946), 84-96.

the logic of his own critical vocabulary. So in reading Dryden's criticism of his plays we must be conscious of the implications of his critical language which he may not have intended, or indeed of which he may not have been aware.

With these provisos in mind then—Dryden's self-justification, his inclination to submit his theoretical commitments to the demands of his practice, and the limitations and latent ambiguities of his critical vocabulary—we may now turn to his remarks on the rhymed heroic play.

(ii) The epic analogy

The basis of Dryden's criticism of heroic drama seems to be his belief that *"an Heroick Play ought to be an imitation, in little of an Heroick Poem."*[10] He makes this claim again and again, and in various ways. In the dedication of *The Rival Ladies* (1664) he justifies the use of rhyme on stage by citing the precedent, among others, of John Denham's *Cooper's Hill*, a long descriptive poem in heroic verse which he calls an "Epick." In the dedication of *The Indian Emperour* (1667) he uses the name, "heroick play," and continued to use it until he stopped writing rhymed plays.[11] In *Of Dramatick Poesie* (1668) he specifically compares tragedy and the epic: "The Genus of them is the same, a just and lively Image of humane nature, in its Actions, Passions, and traverses of Fortune: so is the end, namely for the delight and benefit of Mankind. The Characters and Persons are still the same, *viz.* the greatest of both sorts, onely the manner of acquainting us with those Actions, Passions and Fortunes is different. Tragedy performs it

---

[10] Preface to *The Conquest of Granada* (1672), sig. a3; IV, 21.

[11] For a discussion of the development of this term see W. S. Clark, "The Definition of the 'Heroic Play' in the Restoration Period," *RES*, VIII (1932), 437-44.

viva voce, or by action, in Dialogue, wherein it excels the Epique Poem which does it chiefly by narration, and therefore is not so lively an Image of Humane Nature. However, the agreement betwixt them is such, that if Rhyme be proper for one, it must be for the other." (p. 67; XV, 370) He offers a similar though less explicit justification of rhyme in "A Defence of an Essay of Dramatique Poesie" (1668), asserting that the aim of serious drama is "to move admiration" (the traditional end of epic poetry), for which "a bare imitation will not serve."[12] Similarly, in justifying the astral and aerial spirits in *Tyrannick Love* (1670) he writes: *"Whether there are such Beings or not, it concerns not me; 'tis sufficient for my purpose, that many have believed the affirmative: and that these Heroick Representations, which are of the same Nature with the Epick, are not limited, but with the extremest bounds of what is credible."*

In the preface and dedication of *The Conquest of Granada* (1672) Dryden exploits the "nature" of the epic as the foundation for a full-fledged theory of serious drama. He acknowledges in the preface that the *"first light"* of *"Heroick Plays"* in England came from Sir William Davenant, who in *The Siege of Rhodes* laid the *"excellent ground-work"* for its development. He then adds: *"Having done him this justice, as my guide; I may do my self so much, as to give an account of what I have perform'd after him. I observ'd then . . . what was wanting to the perfection of his* Siege of Rhodes: *which was design, and variety of Characters. And in the midst of this consideration, by meer accident, open'd the next Book that lay by me, which was an* Ariosto *in*

---

[12] *The Indian Emperour,* 2d ed. (1668), sig. A5v; II, 295. "A Defence" was prefaced to the second edition of *The Indian Emperour.*

Italian; *and the very first two lines of that Poem gave me light to all I could desire.*

Le Donne, I Cavalier, L'arme, gli amori,
Le Cortesie, l'audace imprese jo canto, &c.

for the very next reflection which I made was this, That an Heroick Play ought to be an imitation, in little of an Heroick Poem: and, consequently, that Love and Valour ought to be the Subject of it. Both these, Sir William D'Avenant *had begun to shadow: but it was so, as first Discoverers draw their Maps, with headlands, and Promontories, and some few out-lines of somewhat taken at a distance, and which the designer saw not clearly. The common* Drama *oblig'd him to a Plot well-form'd and pleasant, or, as the Antients call'd it, one entire and great Action: but this he afforded not himself in a story, which he neither fill'd with Persons, nor beautified with Characters, nor varied with Accidents. The Laws of an Heroick Poem did not dispence with those of the other, but rais'd them to a greater height: and indulg'd him a farther liberty of Fancy, and of drawing all things as far above the ordinary proportion of the Stage, as that is beyond the common words and actions of humane life: and therefore, in the scanting of his Images, and design, he comply'd not enough with the greatness and Majesty of an Heroick Poem."* (sigs. [a3]-a3v; IV, 19-21)

This definition is stressed by Dryden throughout the preface to *The Conquest of Granada.* After discussing Davenant he repeats again that he has *"modell'd* [his] *Heroique Playes by the Rules of an Heroique Poem,"* and just as in his earlier prefaces he had justified the use of rhyme by such rules, he here defends his stage effects and heroic characterizations. To those who objected to his *"frequent use of Drums and Trumpets,"* and to his *"representations of Battels,"* he answers *"that these war-*

*like Instruments, and, even the representations of fight-
ing on the Stage, are no more than necessary to produce
the effects of an Heroick Play. that is, to raise the
imagination of the Audience, and to perswade them, for
the time, that what they behold on the* Theater *is really
perform'd. The Poet is, then, to endeavour an absolute
dominion over the minds of the Spectators: for, though
our fancy will contribute to its own deceipt, yet a Writer
ought to help its operation."* (sigs. a4v-(*b*); IV, 24-25)
Similarly, to those who objected to Almanzor, Dryden
replies, *"the first Image I had of him was from the*
Achilles *of* Homer, *the next from* Tasso's Rinaldo,
(*who was a copy of the former*:) *and the third from the*
Artaban *of* Monsieur Calprenede: (*who has imitated
both*.)." (sig. (*b*); IV, 26) Dryden then argues that the
qualities and actions of Almanzor that had been most
criticized—his impetuous temper, his changing of sides,
and his performance of alleged impossibilities—are all
to be found and sanctioned in the sources which he has
mentioned. A similar justification of Almanzor is repeated in the dedication of the play: "I have form'd a
Heroe," Dryden writes, "I confess, not absolutely perfect: but of an excessive and overboyling courage. but
Homer and *Tasso* are my precedents. both the Greek
and the Italian Poet had well consider'd that a tame
Heroe who never transgresses the bounds of moral
vertue, would shine but dimly in an Epick poem. the
strictness of those Rules might well give precepts to the
Reader, but would administer little of occasion to the
writer." (sig. *4v; IV, 16)[13]

[13] The preface and dedication of *The Conquest of Granada* are
the last essays in which Dryden shows concern for the epic analogues
of drama. In the dedication of *Aureng-Zebe* (1676), his last rhymed
play, he mentions that the characters of the play *"are the nearest to
those of an Heroick Poem"* (sig. A4v; V, 197), but the reference
is perfunctory and overshadowed by his repudiation of rhyme and
his discussion of his hopes of writing an actual epic poem.

In the light of Dryden's theory, then, it certainly seems plausible to treat his rhymed plays as the dramatic equivalents of the epic poem. Many modern critics, including Dryden's most recent editors, have done so, arguing that Dryden saw the value of the epic idea from Davenant's example, as he himself acknowledges, and that the novelty and most of the salient features of his plays can be explained by his intention to achieve an epic effect, including elevated language and verse, heightened plots and stage effects, and Herculean heroes.[14] These arguments are persuasive but I think, for several reasons, that they ought to be questioned, or at least carefully qualified.

First and most important, the genesis of Dryden's heroic plays, in practice, as we shall see, is extremely eclectic. The plays are greatly indebted to Beaumont and Fletcher's tragicomedies and to Jacobean and Caroline court drama, and they also reveal the influence of French romances, and possibly, as I shall try to show, of Cornélian drama.[15] The epic idea may have helped Dry-

[14] The two most recent arguments for the epic basis of Dryden's heroic plays are John H. Smith and Dougald MacMillan, eds., *The Works of John Dryden*, vol. VIII (Berkeley and Los Angeles, 1962), pp. 287-89; and Eugene M. Waith, *The Herculean Hero* (New York, 1962), pp. 152-201. See also B. J. Pendlebury, *Dryden's Heroic Plays* (London, 1923), *passim*; A. E. Parsons, "The English Heroic Play," *MLR*, XXXIII (1938), 1-14; Reuben A. Brower, "Dryden's Epic Manner and Virgil," *PMLA*, LV (1940), 119-38; Trustan W. Russell, *Voltaire, Dryden and Heroic Tragedy* (New York, 1946), p. 9; and Charles A. McLaughlin, "The English Heroic Play" (unpublished Ph.D. dissertation, University of Chicago, 1957), pp. 106-41.

[15] Scholarly opinion on the sources of heroic drama is quite diverse. Herbert W. Hill, "La Calprenède's Romances and the Restoration Drama," *University of Nevada Studies*, II (1910), 1-56, III (1911), 57-158, and William S. Clark, "The Sources of the Restoration Heroic Play," *RES*, IV (1928), 49-63, argue for the French romances as a principal source of the English heroic play; J. W. Tupper, "The Relation of the Heroic Play to the Romances of Beaumont and Fletcher," *PMLA*, XX (1905), 584-621, stresses Beaumont and

den to assimilate these various sources but it still cannot serve as a single synoptic explanation of the plays. Furthermore, though we may justly ascribe a major role in the origination of the heroic idea to Davenant, the ascription itself merely begs the question, since we are still obliged to understand the many forces which co-operated in producing *The Siege of Rhodes.*

The final proof of these objections must await an analysis of Dryden's plays, which is the object of later chapters of this study. But another reason for qualifying Dryden's emphasis upon the epic, which can be more fully discussed now, lies in the provisos already suggested for reading his criticism. It should be apparent that Dryden frequently invokes epic analogies as a means of defending himself. An allusion to epic authority serves him as a ready-made and critically respectable justification for anything which his critics had found to castigate. Thus he caps his long quarrel over rhyme and figurative language by asserting that an epic play demands epic language; he distinguishes his stage effects from those of the Red Bull writers by claiming that he wishes to find a visual equivalent for the astonishment that is produced by an epic poem; and he defends Almanzor as the lineal descendant of the wrathful Achilles. Now it is perfectly possible that these arguments are also accurate and straightforward statements of aims which Dryden tried to embody in his drama; this would seem partly true of his concept of the hero. But it is

---

Fletcher's influence; Kathleen Lynch, "Conventions of Platonic Drama in the Heroic Plays of Orrery and Dryden," *PMLA*, XLIV (1929), 456-71, points out the persistence of Caroline Platonic conventions in the heroic play; Alfred Harbage, *Cavalier Drama* (New York, 1936), pp. 48-71, outlines the conventions of Cavalier drama found in the Restoration heroic play; C. G. Child, "The Rise of the Heroic Play," *MLN*, XIX (1904), 166-73, and Cornell M. Dowlin, *Sir William Davenant's "Gondibert"* (Philadelphia, 1934) argue for Davenant's role in founding the heroic play upon English dramatic conventions.

also possible that some of these statements are *ad hoc* defenses of facets of his plays that evolved for different reasons and perhaps with different intentions.

The claim, after all, that the heroic play is *"an imitation, in little of an Heroick Poem"* is an *analogy* as much as it is a definition, as much a way of talking about tragedy as it is a substantive theory. To nearly two centuries of English criticism the epic was the highest of the genres, the one which in its ends subsumed all others, and critics spoke of it, as Ian Jack has remarked, in the same way that recent French writers spoke of "la poésie pure."[16] "A HEROICK Poem, truly such," Dryden wrote in the dedication of the *Aeneis* (1697), "is undoubtedly the greatest Work which the Soul of Man is capable to perform." (sig. (a); XIV, 129) The consequence of such a generic hierarchy was that heroic poetry became almost a hypnotic metaphor of serious achievement, and the laws of the epic and the critical apparatus used to describe them became a means of formulating and measuring accomplishment in any genre. The writers of French romances commonly justified the principles of construction and the subject matter of their works by *"the Laws of an Heroick Poem"*;[17] and over half a century later Fielding did the same in his formulation of the theory of the "comic epic in prose."[18] Scudéry's preface to *Ibrahim* (1641), Dryden's preface to *The Conquest of Granada* (1672), and Fielding's preface to *Joseph Andrews* (1742) all

[16] *Augustan Satire* (Oxford, 1952), p. 5.

[17] See citations from the prefaces to French romances in Arthur L. Cooke, "Henry Fielding and the Writers of Heroic Romance," *PMLA*, LXII (1947), 984-94.

[18] Other examples of the use of epic analogies could be cited. One of particular interest is Henry Howard's commendatory verse in the 1647 Beaumont and Fletcher folio, sig. av, which compares Fletcherian characters with famous epic figures. Arbaces and Tigranes, for example, are contrasted with Homer's Achilles.

[14]

proceed on similar principles of argumentation and all appeal to epic precedents; yet the works which they introduce are disparate in construction, style, and content. All three writers were at least partly in search of a critical language which could describe their innovations, and they turned to epic theory because it was most developed and most respected. But their theory must certainly be differentiated from their practice; their real debts to the epic—or to epic theory—are not inclusive.

Dryden's epic analogy, then, is in large measure an argumentative strategy, and once we recognize it as such we can understand his theory better and form a more just estimate of the place of his ideas in English theatrical criticism. For most elements of his theory are more traditional than his argument suggests and his innovations are frequently the cause, rather than the consequence, of his use of the epic analogy. With this perspective we may now examine Dryden's treatment of structure, staging, and style. His concept of the heroic hero will be considered in the following chapter.

(iii) Structure and staging

As we have seen, in the preface to *The Conquest of Granada* Dryden accuses Davenant of the *"scanting of his Images, and design"* in *The Siege of Rhodes* in a *"story, which he neither fill'd with Persons, nor beautified with Characters, nor varied with Accidents"*; and he implies that he has remedied Davenant's defects by following *"the Laws of an Heroick Poem."* In fact, however, nothing could be further from the truth. Dryden's reference to the epic in this instance is almost deliberately misleading, for his conception of the plot of a heroic play is entirely derivative, the product of a half century of thought on dramatic structure.

His most revealing statements about plot occur before the heyday of *The Conquest of Granada*. In the dedication of *The Rival Ladies* (1664) he writes: "*He may be allow'd sometimes to Err, who undertakes to move so many Characters and Humours as are requisite in a Play, in those narrow Channels which are proper to each of them: To conduct his imaginary Persons, through so many various Intrigues and Chances, as the Labouring Audience shall think them lost under every Billow; and then at length to work them so naturally out of their Distresses, that when the whole Plot is laid open, the Spectators may rest satisfied, that every cause was powerfull enough to produce the effect it had; and that the whole Chain of them was with such due order Linck'd together, that the first Accident would naturally beget the second, till they all render'd the Conclusion necessary.*" (sig. A2; II, 130) Dryden uses similar terms a few years later in *Of Dramatick Poesie* (1668). Speaking of the four parts of a play, a division which he wrongly attributes to Aristotle, Eugenius remarks: "First, The *Protasis* or entrance, which gives light onely to the Characters of the persons, and proceeds very little into any part of the action: 2ly, The *Epitasis*, or working up of the Plot where the Play grows warmer: the design or action of it is drawing on, and you see something promising that it will come to pass: Thirdly, the *Catastasis*, or Counterturn, which destroys that expectation, imbroyles the action in new difficulties, and leaves you far distant from that hope in which it found you, as you may have observ'd in a violent stream resisted by a narrow passage; it runs round to an eddy, and carries back the waters with more swiftness then it brought them on: Lastly, the *Catastrophe*, which the Grecians call'd [λύσις], the French *le denouement*, and we the discovery or unravelling of the Plot: there you see all things setling again upon their first foundations, and the obstacles which hindred the design or action of the Play once remov'd, it ends with that resemblance of truth and nature, that the audience are satisfied with the conduct of it." (p. 16; XV, 303-04)

Neither of these statements is novel, still less are they the result of Dryden's professed desire to imitate the epic in his tragedies. Both the concept of plot and the terms used to describe it are traditional. Davenant himself had made similar observations many times. Indeed in the preface to *The Siege of Rhodes* (1656), the play which Dryden criticized for its *"scanting of . . . Images, and design,"* Davenant had explained that because of the limitations of actors and of the physical stage in the Commonwealth production, the reader necessarily could not "expect the chief Ornaments belonging to a History Drammatically digested into Turns and Counter-turns, to double Walks, and interweavings of design"; and several years earlier, in the preface to *Gondibert* (1651) he described what he considered to be the traditional structure of the "regular species" of English drama in similar terms: "The first *Act* is the general preparative, by rendring the chiefest characters of persons, and ending with something that looks like an obscure promise of design. The second begins with an introducement of new persons, so finishes all the characters, and ends with some little performance of that design which was promis'd at the parting of the first *Act*. The third makes a visible correspondence in the under-walks (or lesser intrigues) of persons; and ends with an ample turn of the main design, and expectation of a new. The fourth (ever having occasion to be the longest) gives a notorious turn to all the under-walks, and a counterturn to that main design which was chang'd in the third. The fifth begins with an intire diversion of the main, and dependant Plotts; then makes the general correspondence of the persons more discernable, and ends with an easy untying of those particular knots, which made a contexture of the whole; leaving such satisfaction of probabilities with the Spectator, as may perswade him that neither Fortune in the fate of the Persons, nor the Writer in the Representment, have been unnatural or exorbitant." (pp. 23-4)[19]

The correspondences between Dryden's discussion of plot and these passages is unmistakable: "design" for both men involves peripatetic action and a complicated intrigue (including sub-plots and an artful catastrophe and denouement). Dryden was obviously indebted to Davenant for these views, but it must be reiterated that neither in Davenant's case nor his was the idea of a heroic plot born of epic rules. Davenant was one of the most versatile professional playwrights of the seventeenth century and the dramatic construction which he recommends was the result of his experience on the Jacobean and Caroline stage. His concept of structure was a codification of critical ideals which had reigned uninterrupted since the time of Jonson, who had first formulated them clearly and given them his authority. There is nothing in Davenant's theory of structure—or Dryden's—that cannot be found in Jonson or in intervening writers and critics.[20]

[19] Davenant made a number of similar statements both before and after the Restoration. See the epilogue to *The First Day's Entertainment at Rutland-House* (1656) and "Poem to the King's Most Sacred Majesty" (1663) in *The Works of Sr William D'avenant Kt* (1673), section one, pp. 359 and 269, respectively.

[20] For Jonson's discussions of plot see especially *Every Man out of his Humour* and *The Magnetick Lady* in *Ben Jonson*, eds. Herford and Simpson, 11 vols. (Oxford, 1925-52), III, 521-22, 562; VI, 512, 527, 563-64, 578. Jonson's reputation in the seventeenth century was very great and his ideas on dramatic structure were essentially duplicated by later writers. See, *e.g.*, William Cartwright's elegy of Jonson, Herford, and Simpson, XI, 456; James Shirley's preface to *Comedies and Tragedies Written by Francis Beavmont and Iohn Fletcher Gentleman* (1647), sig. A3v; Cartwright's elegy to Fletcher, *ibid.*, sig. [d2]; and M. Lluelin's elegy of Cartwright, *Comedies, Tragi-Comedies, With other Poems, by Mr. William Cartwright* (1651), sig. [*18].

[18]

The heroic "story," therefore, which Dryden extols in the preface to *The Conquest of Granada*, a story *"fill'd with Persons, . . . beautified with Characters, . . . varied with Accidents,"* is traditional, the inheritance of a half century of English drama and criticism. Occasionally, when he was freed of his own polemical rhetoric, Dryden realized this himself. In *Of Dramatick Poesie* he praised both Jonson and Fletcher for their structural legacies to subsequent English dramatists, and he analyzed the "admirable plot" of Jonson's *Silent Woman* at length, as the pattern of a perfect play. In a generous moment he even conceded Davenant's skill in "contrivance."[21]

Dryden's apparently revolutionary concept of the staging of heroic plays is similarly indebted to the criticism and practice of his predecessors. Drums, trumpets, battle scenes, and opulent scenery invariably accompanied his plays, and he often calls attention to them. In the prologue to *The Rival Ladies* he points out:

> *You now have Habits, Dances, Scenes, and Rhymes;*
> *High Language often; I, and Sense, sometimes.*

In the epilogue to *The Indian Queen* (1665) he remarks:

> *You see what Shifts we are inforc'd to try*
> *To help out Wit with some Variety;*
> *Shows may befound* [sic] *that never yet were seen,*
> *'Tis hard to finde such Wit as ne're has been: . . .*
> *'Tis true, y'have marks enough, the Plot, the Show,*
> *The Poets Scenes, nay, more, the Painters too.*

[21] For Dryden's discussion of Jonson see *Of Dramatick Poesie*, pp. 46-56; XV, 346-55; for his commendation of Davenant, see the preface to *The Tempest* (1670). Cf. Dryden's treatment of the catastrophe and denouement, *Of Dramatick Poesie*, pp. 16, 53; XV, 303-04, 351-52, and Jonson's treatment, Herford and Simpson, VI, 527, 578.

Indeed, the scenery of *The Indian Queen* was apparently so popular (and expensive) that Dryden wrote a sequel in order that it could be used again. He mentions in the prologue to *The Indian Emperour* (1665) that

> *The Scenes are old, the Habits are the same*
> *We wore last year, before the Spaniards came.*

Dryden seems to have been pointing out what was already sufficiently apparent to his audience. Evelyn noted in his account of *The Indian Queen* that "the like" of the scenery and decorations "had never ben seene here as happly (except rarely any where else) on a mercenarie *Theater*."[22] Evelyn's comment, however, is relatively objective. Dryden's more hostile critics almost invariably derided the scenic extravagance of his plays.[23] In the preface to *The Conquest of Granada* Dryden defended himself, as we have seen, by claiming that his stage devices were *"no more than necessary to produce the effects of an Heroick Play. that is, to raise the imagination of the Audience, and to perswade them, for the time, that what they behold on the* Theater *is really perform'd."* In the dedication of *Amboyna* (1673), Dryden wrote more specifically of admiration: " 'Tis that noble Passion, to which *Poets* raise their Audience in highest Subjects, and they have then gain'd over them the greatest Victory, when they are Ravish'd into a Pleasure, which is not to be express'd by Words." (sig. A2v; V, 5) But Dryden's association of this epic pleasure with the spectacle of tragedy is less radical than he makes it appear. The rhetorical aim of *moving* an audience was an obvious as well as orthodox feature of earlier English

[22] *The Diary*, ed. E. S. de Beer, 6 vols. (Oxford, 1955), III, 368-69.

[23] See, *e.g.*, Edward Howard, *The Six Days Adventure* (1671), preface, sigs. A4v, a; *The Rehearsal*, IV, i, pp. 38-39; *The Censure of the Rota*, p. 3; and [Joseph Arrowsmith], *The Reformation* (1673), prologue, and IV, i, p. 48.

theatrical criticism. Jonson had noted that the just critic would appreciate how an author " . . . doth raigne in mens affections; how invade, and breake in upon them; and makes their minds like the thing he writes"; and James Shirley, in common with many other critics, had praised Fletcher for raising passions *"to that excellent pitch and by such insinuating degrees that you shall not chuse but consent, & go along with them, finding your self at last grown insensibly the very same person you read. . . ."*[24]

Dryden's reasoning in justifying stage spectacle, therefore, is traditional. And what is equally important, it came after the fact. His attention to scenery was a response to a theatrical development that had probably begun with the introduction of the devices of the masque into English court drama. As early as 1639 Davenant, who had had experience with both masques and court plays, had contemplated the construction of a new theater in London which would allow him to exploit such devices for a popular audience; and, as Nethercot points out,[25] one of the elements Davenant always stressed in his own court drama was his "scenes"— including the effects of perspective, painted settings, and mechanical contrivances. Davenant probably had these plans in mind when he apologized in the preface to *The Siege of Rhodes* for the meagerness of his scenes and argument. In any case, Davenant had written masques and made his plans for a new theater long before he had written *Gondibert* or its preface; and there is thus little reason for assuming that either his use of the epic analogy, or Dryden's, was responsible for the peculiarly operatic effects of heroic drama. It is far more likely that the process worked in reverse, that with both men, the

[24] Herford and Simpson, VIII, 588; preface to Beaumont and Fletcher, *Comedies and Tragedies* (1647), sig. A3v.

[25] Arthur H. Nethercot, *Sir William D'avenant* (Chicago, 1938), p. 169.

plays (and their accompanying critical justifications) were at least partly designed to accommodate a maximum use of scenery.

(iv) Rhyme

Allardyce Nicoll has argued that rhyme was an adventitious feature of the heroic play and has pointed out that after the decline of rhyme, many of the characteristics of heroic drama remained on the English stage.[26] This is true, but in Dryden's case, misleading. There is ample evidence to show that for Dryden rhyme and figurative expression were at the heart of heroic drama and that when he abandoned rhyme he also abandoned the idea of the heroic play as he had originally conceived it.

The testimony of his contemporaries is clear on this point. His critics uniformly regarded his verse and his disposition for rhyme and figurative writing as central features of his heroic plays. His rhyme and heroical similes were criticized not only by Sir Robert Howard, as we shall see shortly, but by a host of other writers as well. Edward Howard joined his brother in condemning Dryden's rhyme, and Shadwell registered his disapproval of heroes who *still resolve to live and die in Rhime,*" and who *"Fight, and wooe in Verse in the same breath, / And make Similitudes, and Love in Death."*[27] After the appearance of *The Conquest of Granada,* such attacks multiplied. Buckingham pilloried Dryden's rhymes and similes throughout *The Rehearsal;* Edward Ravenscroft's prologue to *The Citizen Turn'd Gentleman* (1672) mentioned the vogue for *"Playes of Rhyme and Noyse with wond'rous show";* Richard Leigh's *The Censure of the Rota* (1673) harped on Dryden's dependence

---

[26] *Restoration Drama* (Cambridge, 1955), pp. 100-02.
[27] Howard, *The Womens Conquest* (1671), sigs. [A4]-A4v; Shadwell, the prologue to *The Sullen Lovers* (1668).

upon rhyme, and sarcastically included an appendix of
rhetorical figures serviceable for all occasions (pp. 16, 18,
19-20); and the ironical prescription for a heroic play
in *The Reformation* (1673), a play attributed to Joseph
Arrowsmith, noted as a *sine qua non* that "you put your
story into rime. . . ." (IV, i, p. 48) Even after Dryden
had abandoned the rhymed heroic play, the memory of
his sins of rhyme and simile persisted. *The Medal of
John Bayes* (1682), which was a vicious attack upon
Dryden, grudgingly admitted that he had had "a kind
of Excellence in Rime," but delighted that "Rime's sad
downfal" had brought his ruin (pp. 4, 5); and the Earl
of Mulgrave, though one of Dryden's most dependable
patrons, could not refrain in *An Essay on Poetry* (1682)
from castigating the plays of the past decade where
"Figures of *Speech"* had usurped the genuine language
of passion, and where men had died "in Simile," and
lived "in Rime." (pp. 12, 13)

These comments are unmistakably confirmed in Dryden's own criticism. As he develops his theory of the
heroic play in his early essays, the championship of
rhyme and figurative expression is his central concern,
and provides the focus for his treatment of a wide range
of problems. His first discussion of rhyme appears in
the dedication of *The Rival Ladies*. He remarks that
*"the Excellence and Dignity of it, were never fully
known till Mr.* Waller *taught it; He first made writing
easily an Art: First shew'd us to conclude the Sense,
most commonly, in Distichs; which in the Verse of those
before him, runs on for so many Lines together, that the
Reader is out of Breath to overtake it. This sweetness of
Mr.* Wallers Lyrick *Poesie was afterwards follow'd in
the Epick by Sir* John Denham, *in his* Coopers-Hill: *a
Poem which your Lordship knows for the Majesty of the
Style, is, and ever will be the exact Standard of good
Writing. But if we owe the Invention of it to Mr.*

[23]

Waller, *we are acknowledging for the Noblest use of it to Sir* William D'avenant; *who at once brought it upon the Stage, and made it perfect, in the Siege of* Rhodes." (sig. [A4]; II, 137) Having established the literary excellence of this form of verse, and its attendant dignity and majesty, Dryden then—and only then—considers the subjects which are appropriate to it. He acknowledges the common objection that *"Rhyme is only an Embroidery of Sence, to make that which is ordinary in it self pass for excellent with less Examination,"* but he concludes that such a defect is caused by an abuse of rhyme: *"as the best Medicines may lose their Virtue, by being ill applied, so is it with Verse, if a fit Subject be not chosen for it. Neither must the Argument alone, but the Characters, and Persons be great and noble; Otherwise, (as* Scaliger *says of* Claudian) *the Poet will be,* Ignobiliore materiâ depressus. *The Scenes, which, in my Opinion, most commend it, are those of Argumentation and Discourse, on the result of which the doing or not doing some considerable action should depend."* (sig. A4v; II, 138-39) T. S. Eliot has suggested that Dryden defended the rhymed couplet "because it was the form of verse which came most natural to him,"[28] and the suggestion is persuasive. The argument of the dedication to *The Rival Ladies* reads suspiciously as if Dryden were trying to translate his instinct for rhyme into a total theory of drama; all the salient features of his later theory are present, even the epic analogy, which is implied in the reference to Denham's *Cooper's Hill.* But in any case, the essay stresses the literary perfection of verse which had been practiced by Denham and Waller and ennobled on the stage by Davenant, and its argument is controlled throughout by the principle of decorum of style. At its inception, therefore, Dryden's

[28] *John Dryden* (New York, 1932), p. 37.

[24]

theory of the heroic play constituted a commitment to rhyme and an exploration of the subjects suitable to it.

The following year, in the preface to *Four New Plays* (1665), Sir Robert Howard objected to rhymed drama, arguing that since a play, unlike a poem, "*is presented as the present Effect of Accidents not thought of*," rhymed verse and rhymed repartee were unnatural, appearing rather as the premeditation of the author than as the natural result of the dialogue and conversation of characters. He added that "*the dispute is not which way a Man may write best in, but which is most proper for the Subject he writes upon. . . .*" (sig. [a4]) In *Of Dramatick Poesie* (1668) Crites reiterates Howard's position, offering a series of arguments terminating in the assertion that since people do not speak in rhyme and since drama must imitate the conversation of people, rhyme has no place in serious drama. Crites recommends that blank verse, which is "nearest Nature," should be preferred. Neander's response is an appeal to decorum: "I answer you . . . by distinguishing betwixt what is nearest to the nature of Comedy, which is the imitation of common persons and ordinary speaking, and what is nearest the nature of a serious Play: this last is indeed the representation of Nature, but 'tis Nature wrought up to an higher pitch. The Plot, the Characters, the Wit, the Passions, the Descriptions, are all exalted above the level of common converse, as high as the imagination of the Poet can carry them, with proportion to verisimility. Tragedy we know is wont to image to us the minds and fortunes of noble persons, and to portray these exactly, Heroick Rhime is nearest Nature, as being the noblest kind of modern verse." (p. 66; XV, 369) As in the dedication of *The Rival Ladies* the burden of Dryden's argument lies in his insistence that the style be suited to the purpose of the genre. Thus, a serious play is "nearest Nature" when, in certain respects, it is

[25]

farthest from it; decorum, not realism, is the measure of artistic perfection. As Dryden explains, "A Play ... to be like Nature, is to be set above it; as Statues which are plac'd on high are made greater then the life, that they may descend to the sight in their just proportion" (p. 67; XV, 370); and the artifice of rhyme, "the noblest kind of modern verse," is the means by which this aesthetic distance can best be achieved.

When these passages appeared in print Dryden had already virtually defined "heroick plays" as those which employed verse. In the dedication of *The Indian Emperour* (1667) he mentions the approbation of heroic plays at court, and adds that *"The most eminent persons for Wit and Honour in the Royal Circle having so far own'd them, that they have judg'd no way so fit as Verse to entertain a Noble Audience, or to express a noble passion."* The conjunction of verse and heroic drama is also unmistakable in "A Defence of an Essay of Dramatique Poesie," which Dryden added to the second edition of *The Indian Emperour* (1668). Howard had repeated his objections to rhyme in the preface to *The Duke of Lerma*, and Dryden replies with a searching exposition of his belief that above all "a Play is suppos'd to be the work of the Poet." In support of this conviction he argues that " 'Tis true that to imitate well is a Poets [sic] work; but to affect the Soul, and excite the Passions, and above all to move admiration (which is the delight of serious Plays) a bare imitation will not serve. The converse therefore which a Poet is to imitate, must be heighten'd with all the Arts and Ornaments of Poesie; and must be such, as, strictly consider'd, could never be supposed spoken by any without premeditation." (sig. A5v; II, 295) This passage provides further evidence that in Dryden's mind the heroic play was inseparable from "all the Arts and Ornaments of Poesie," and that indeed his stipulation of epic admiration as the end of heroic drama may have been a means of guaranteeing the practice of such arts and ornaments.

In the preface to *The Conquest of Granada* Dryden once again justifies rhyme—this time confident that it is *"already in possession of the Stage."* He remarks that *"it is very clear to all, who understand Poetry, that serious Playes ought not to imitate Conversation too nearly. If nothing were to be rais'd above that level, the foundation of Poetry would be destroy'd. and, if you once admit of a Latitude, that thoughts may be exalted, and that Images and Actions may be rais'd above the life, and describ'd in measure without Rhyme, that leads you insensibly, from your own Principles to mine: You are already so far onward of your way, that you have forsaken the imitation of ordinary converse. You are gone beyond it; and, to continue where you are, is to lodge in the open field, betwixt two Inns. You have lost that which you call natural, and have not acquir'd the last perfection of Art. But it was onely custome which cozen'd us so long: we thought, because* Shakespear *and* Fletcher *went no farther, that there the Pillars of Poetry were to be erected. That, because they excellently describ'd Passion without Rhyme, therefore Rhyme was not capable of describing it."* (sigs. a2-a2v; IV, 18-19)

Rhymed heroic verse, *"the last perfection of Art,"* is clearly the vital center of Dryden's theory of the heroic play; and it makes sense that it should be. Towards the close of his career, Dryden said of his contribution to the language and poetry of his country: "Somewhat (give me leave to say) I have added to both of them in the choice of *Words*, and Harmony of Numbers which were wanting, especially the last, in all our Poets, even in those who being endu'd with Genius, yet have not Cultivated their Mother-Tongue with sufficient Care; or relying on the Beauty of their Thoughts, have judg'd the Ornament of Words, and sweetness of Sound unnecessary."[29] The mixture of pride and humility in this statement indicates how deeply he meant it, and only a disposition which regards such matters as trivial can prevent us from seeing the importance of his concern with language and versification throughout his criticism. Dryden considers all aspects of dramatic art—structure, staging, and characterizations included—but from first to last his criticism of the drama reveals an extraordinary attention to language and expression. His preference for the writing over the plotting of plays was profound and unalterable. The discussion of the question in the preface to *Secret-Love* (1668) is typical. Dryden notes that the comedy is regular, "according to the strictest of Dramatick Laws," but that he does not value himself upon its correctness, "because with all that symmetry of pa[rt]s, it may want an air and spirit (which consists in the writing) to set it off." The priority of the "air and spirit (which consists in the writing)" is evident in Dryden's practice as well. In *The Rehearsal*, when Bayes is called upon to defend his lagging plot, he explains impatiently: "Plot stand still! why, what a Devil is the Plot good for, but to bring in fine things?" (III, i, p. 22) The satire is just. Dryden was always interested in "fine things" in his plays: *the descriptions, similitudes, and propriety of Language*," which gave a play its "*life-touches*" and "*secret graces*"; the "*propriety of thoughts and words*," which were its "*hidden beauties*"; the "*Descriptions, Images, Similitudes, and Moral Sentences*," which were its "*most poetical parts*."[30]

Part of the reason for Dryden's preference for these "*most poetical parts*" is that he was never entirely con-

[29] Postscript to the *Aeneis* (1697).
[30] Prefaces to *An Evening's Love* (1671); *The Spanish Fryar* (1681); and *Don Sebastian* (1690), respectively. For an illuminating discussion of Dryden's views of mimesis in the drama, see Moody Prior, "Poetic Drama: an Analysis and a Suggestion," *English Institute Essays 1949* (New York, 1950), pp. 10-16.

tent as a dramatist. Even at the beginning of his career he disparaged his talent for comedy, and when his contact with the stage became more intermittent he expressed dissatisfaction not only with his audiences but with the nature of the stage itself. While repudiating the verbal extravagance of his earlier plays in the dedication of *The Spanish Fryar* (1681) he notes that *"as 'tis my Interest to please my Audience, so 'tis my Ambition to be read; that I am sure is the more lasting and the nobler Design: for the propriety of thoughts and words, which are the hidden beauties of a Play, are but confus'dly judg'd in the vehemence of Action."* Elsewhere he speaks of his *"loathing"* of the stage, and implies that all his plays except *All for Love* were acts of compromise, "given to the people."[31] After he had severed all connections with the theater, he confessed that his "Genius never much inclin'd" him to the stage.[32] Some of these statements may be written off as temporary pique or disenchantment, but not all of them. A comparison of Dryden's criticism with Corneille's on this point is instructive. Corneille quarrels with his critics but rarely with his materials, and he never patronizes the physical theater. What is more, he never makes a disjunction between the expression and the action of drama in the first place. Dryden's disposition to do just this suggests that notwithstanding his practical mastery of all the elements of his craft he approached playwriting with consciously literary pretensions: his preoccupations were primarily verbal.[33]

[31] Preface to *Don Sebastian*; and preface to *The Art of Painting* (1695), p. liv; XVII, 333.
[32] Dedication of *The Satires of Juvenal* (1693), p. xiii; XIII, 30.
[33] D. W. Jefferson has treated Dryden's plays on this assumption: see "The Significance of Dryden's Heroic Plays," *Proceedings of the Leeds Philosophical and Literary Society*, V (1940), 125-39, and "Aspects of Dryden's Imagery," *Essays in Criticism*, IV (1954), 20-41. See also Reuben A. Brower, "Dryden's Epic Manner and Virgil," *PMLA*, LV (1940), 119-38.

Paradoxically, this personal bias was amply supported if not caused by similar interests in the previous English aristocratic drama. Jonson, the dramatist who had startled his contemporaries by calling his plays, "works," was, as usual, the first significant source of these interests both in criticism and practice. Jonson believed that a dramatist should italicize his own artifice, "that the studious of elegancy be not defrauded," and the attention to artistic elegance and propriety of style—to what Dryden called *"the hidden beauties of a Play"*—is a hallmark of his criticism.[34] He investigated questions of style at considerable length, and as in the case of his comments on structure his prescriptions exerted a formidable influence on his successors. In their praise of him they singled out the correctness and purity of his style,[35] and in their own practice they formed themselves upon the stylistic ideals which he had tried to teach. Fletcherian tragicomedy and Caroline court drama are both marked by an extreme and self-conscious attention to rhetorical artifice, in Dryden's words, to *"Descriptions, Images, Similitudes, and Moral Sentences."* James Shirley wrote of Beaumont and Fletcher's plays: *"You may here find passions raised to that excellent pitch and by such insinuating degrees that you shall not chuse but consent, & go along with them, finding your self at last grown insensibly the very same person you read, and then stand admiring the subtile Trackes of your engagement."*[36] Fletcherian drama is predicated upon the spectator's consciousness of the rhetoric by which he is engaged—as one scholar has shown, many

[34] Herford and Simpson, VIII, 566-67. See also *ibid.*, III, 10; IV, 350; V, 19, 291; VIII, 588, 621, 626.

[35] See, *e.g.*, comments quoted in Herford and Simpson, XI, 316, 325, 354, 457-58; and in G. E. Bentley, *Shakespeare and Jonson*, 2 vols. (Chicago, 1945), II, 46.

[36] Preface to Beaumont and Fletcher, *Comedies and Tragedies* (1647), sig. A3v.

of the situations in the plays are borrowed directly from Senecan declamations—[37] and the rhetorical indulgences of Caroline court drama need hardly be emphasized. Davenant too shows evidence of this indulgence. It is interesting that he seems to have been noted for a fondness for rhetorical display by his contemporaries. After his death in 1668 a pamphlet was published depicting his trial in the other world, primarily for stylistic offenses. His defense pleads

> . . . for Eloquence
> How never any hyperbolies
> Were higher, or farther stretch'd than his;
>
> Nor ever comparisons again
> Made things compar'd more clear and plain.

Momus, his judge, rejects the plea and replies: "That all his Wit lay in Hyperbolies and Comparisons, which, when Accessory, were commendable enough, but when Principal, deserv'd no great commendations. . . ."[38] In any event Davenant was as inclined to experiment with the verbal aspects of drama as he was with its physical staging. There is evidence, indeed, that he wrote *The Siege of Rhodes* entirely in heroic couplets which he then altered to fit musical requirements;[39] and his reasons for this innovation would seem to anticipate Dryden's very

[37] Eugene M. Waith, *The Pattern of Tragicomedy in Beaumont and Fletcher* (New Haven, 1952), pp. 86-98.

[38] Richard Flecknoe, *Sr William D'avenant's Voyage to the Other World* (1668), sigs. A5v, [A6]. It is interesting that both Davenant and Dryden should have been known for their addiction to figures and similes. *A Journal from Parnassus*, ed. Hugh Macdonald (London, 1937), written in approximately 1688, derides Dryden's disposition for similes in almost the same terms Flecknoe had used two decades earlier to condemn Davenant's love of hyperboles. (pp. 4, 11)

[39] Edward J. Dent, *Foundations of English Opera* (Cambridge, 1928), pp. 65-68.

closely: "In Tragedy," one of the characters in *The Play-house to be Lett* (1663) remarks:

> . . . the language of the Stage
> Is rais'd above the common dialect;
> Our passions rising with the height of Verse.[40]

The self-conscious employment of verbal artifice, therefore, had a long history in early seventeenth-century drama. Dryden was an heir to this tradition and directed his rhymed plays at an aristocratic audience which still appreciated and demanded it. In the early years of the Restoration, when the literary preferences of the Court seem to have dominated the public stage,[41] Jonson enjoyed an almost unquestioned reputation as the arbiter of English dramatic taste, and revivals of Beaumont and Fletcher competed on equal terms with contemporary plays. In *Of Dramatick Poesie,* as we have seen, Dryden praised the "many and profitable rules for perfecting the Stage" which Jonson had left behind in the *Discoveries,* and he also paid homage to the contemporary theatrical success of Beaumont and Fletcher. (pp. 49, 50; XIV, 346, 348)

Dryden wrote in the preface to *Annus Mirabilis* (1667) that he preferred Virgil to Ovid because Virgil, speaking usually in his own person, *"thereby gains more liberty then the other, to express his thoughts with all the graces of elocution, to write more figuratively, and to confess, as well the labour as the force of his imagina-*

---

[40] *The Works* (1673), section two, p. 72.

[41] In the dedication of *The Indian Emperour* (1665), Dryden remarks that *"THE favour which Heroick Plays have lately found upon our Theaters has been wholly deriv'd to them, from the countenance and approbation they have received at Court."* In the "Defence of the Epilogue, or an Essay on the Dramatic Poetry of the Last Age" (1672) Dryden goes even further, claiming that the eminence of contemporary drama is owing in great measure to the access of modern dramatists to the refinement of court conversation. (*Conquest of Granada,* pp. 173-74; IV, 241-42)

[32]

tion." (sig. A8; IX, 97) The rhymed heroic play was Dryden's attempt to bring to perfection upon the English stage a language of tragedy that would "*confess, as well the labour as the force of his imagination.*" His championship of rhyme and figurative expression was at the heart of this attempt and constituted at once his commitment to the tradition of his predecessors and his effort to surpass it. As he remarked in the preface to *The Conquest of Granada*: "... *it was onely custome which cozen'd us so long: we thought, because* Shakespear *and* Fletcher *went no farther, that there the Pillars of Poetry were to be erected. That, because they excellently describ'd Passion without Rhyme, therefore Rhyme was not capable of describing it.*" And he added with unmistakable triumph: "*onely I have us'd it without the mixture of Prose.*" (sigs. a2-a2v; IV, 18-19) When Dryden finally succumbed to blank verse and to the mixture of prose, the orientation of his plays changed markedly, as we shall see when we examine them; and so did the theater for which he was writing. Sentimental drama had perceptibly begun. Audiences increasingly demanded illusion, not artifice, and the aristocratic preoccupations of the earlier drama became more and more remote.

CHAPTER II

The Heroic Hero

THOUGH it is rather unlikely that Dryden came upon the idea of heroic drama *"by meer accident,"* as he asserted, through a casual glance at Ariosto, the influence of heroic myth upon his super-heroes is indisputable. Critics of his plays have long recognized this, and various sources or models for his heroes have been suggested: early in this century, for example, Herbert W. Hill demonstrated the influence of the protagonists of Calprenède's heroic romances (especially Artaban) and quite recently Eugene M. Waith emphasized the tradition of the Herculean hero in the earlier English drama (Tamburlaine, Coriolanus, Antony, and Bussy D'Ambois).[1] Both studies are convincing; Waith's, in addition, provides a fruitful approach for a critical analysis of the plays.

What these studies neglect, however, is a thorough consideration of the peculiarly contemporary features of Dryden's heroes: not merely the ideas which he added to the older traditions, whether of the French romance or of the English stage, but the ideas which made these older traditions viable for the particular audience and milieu of the Restoration stage. The heroic ideal was so widely diffused in the mid-seventeenth century, subsumed so much of the literature of both England and the Continent, that a discussion of Dryden's earlier sources or models runs a great risk of being reductive. What is needed is an understanding of his particular

[1] Hill, "La Calprenède's Romances and the Restoration Drama," *University of Nevada Studies*, II (1910), 1-56; III (1911), 57-158; Waith, *The Herculean Hero* (New York, 1962), pp. 152-201. For other approaches, see above, Chapter I, note 15.

expression of heroism and of the particular circumstances under which it flourished. Two points especially seem to me to deserve an emphasis which they have not usually received: the first is the libertinism of Dryden's heroes, and the second is their resemblance to the protagonists of Cornélian drama.

(i) Libertine heroism

Dryden's rhymed plays were written and performed during the years in which the libertine hero flourished in Restoration comedy: the production of Dryden's first and last rhymed plays coincide almost exactly with the performances of the first and last plays of Sir George Etherege. The same audience saw and presumably applauded the works of both men, and there seems no reason to believe, as many theater historians have, that this audience was uniquely capable (or guilty) of possessing one set of ethical attitudes for tragedy and another set for comedy. The evidence of contemporary reactions to the drama of the period shows precisely the opposite: to the people who saw or read them at the time the theatrical appeal of comedy and tragedy was usually very similar and their moral assumptions seemed compatible. The opposition between an allegedly romantic heroic drama and a realistic comedy of manners, the heroes of the former ideal and idealized, the heroes of the latter natural and naturalistic, is a modern and tendentious distinction.[2]

The testimony of Dryden's contemporaries on this point is illuminating. Dryden's heroic plays aroused considerable controversy—*The Rehearsal* was but one of

[2] Thomas Fujimura, "The Appeal of Dryden's Heroic Plays," *PMLA*, LXXV (1960), 37-45, is one of the few modern critics to argue for a libertine interpretation of Dryden's plays. I cannot, however, endorse all of Fujimura's argument; our differences should emerge from the discussion in section ii of this chapter.

many attacks—and a significant number of these attacks tended to link his tragedies to the comedies of the period and to condemn both for a libertine subversion of orthodox morality. In the early 1670's, for example, a group of pamphlets was published defending marriage against the "heroick extravagance" which was being represented on stage. One pamphlet in particular, *Remarques on the Humours and Conversations of the Town* (1673), launched a full scale offensive against the heroic play. Its author referred sarcastically to the truth of a "late Printed Discourse" (an allusion to the preface to *The Conquest of Granada*) which celebrated "the sufficiency of an excellent Poet, to instruct Mankind in the most important points they ought to believe." (p. 44) He then analyzed the heroic play: "But to look nearer into their pretences; the great thing in which they triumph, is an Heroick Play; which yet is imperfect in that Vertue of which they boast: they have made the three grand characters of a Hero, to be Love, Honour, and Friendship; but to what fantastick heights they have raised these is apparent in their Poems. They have made Love to be the hot passion of an hour; tried by Chymaerical and odd experiments; unpracticable to the World, and rather an Idaea fit to misguide the leisure and the sentiments of Youth, than capable of giving any just assistance to the occasions of Life: he that pretends to instruct, is not to celebrate the things that happen, but the things that ought to be. Their Honour consists in an obstinacy to combate [sic] necessity and time; in maintaining the feiry [sic] ground of Fame; to vanquish Reason and generosity in the contempt of life; gathering the spreading glory of a Hero into a single punctilio. This is their Honour, as much Chymaerical as their Love. Neither is their Friendship less idle, whilst it consists in resigning an adored Mistress; in becoming the confident [sic] of amours; or a Knight

Errant pursuing the capricio of an other; a scruing up the courage of a friend to those fantastick heights, where we can dare to perish with him." (pp. 52-54) Branding the writers of such plays as "the Idolaters of the Heathen Vertue," the author of the *Remarques* criticized "the easie and the vicious humour of an Age" which supported them. (pp. 49, 62) He condemned the prevailing philosophy of Epicurean atomism: " . . . that several Troops and Parties of Atoms . . . did at last under the conduct of chance alone, (for they allow no greater a cause to have commanded in the morning of the Universe.) rendezvous in a most glorious and beautiful World." (pp. 73-4) He deplored the disposition of the Town to subvert the institution of marriage: " . . . they represent, that the slighting of the pleasures of Marriage, is a greatness of Soul, that scorns to be imposed on; but that the pursuing variety of amours, is the peculiar gusto of a great wit: for that is a principle from which they must not recede, that all their extravagancies, are not only the pleasing of their Humours, but inseparable proofs of extraordinary capacities . . . ." (p. 79)

There is, of course, more than a tinge in these strictures of the old Puritan war against the stage, and one of the answers to the *Remarques*, a pamphlet entitled, *Remarks upon Remarques* (1673), accused the author of being "one of the *Rump-Parliament*." (p. 50) But the writer of the same answer nevertheless must have felt that the *Remarques* had successfully impugned contemporary society, for like the good "Modern" he evidently was, he offered a thoroughgoing defense of his culture, accenting particularly advances in commerce, science, and the arts. Significantly, in no instance did he deny the charges of scepticism and libertinism that had been made by the author of the *Remarques*. In any case, it is clear that the author of the *Remarques* associated the libertinism of Restoration comedy with Dryden's heroic plays, and regarded his celebration of Love, Honor, and Friendship as passions inimical to Christian virtue.[3] His assertion, moreover, that the poet "is not to celebrate the things that happen, but the things that ought to be," should suggest strong reservations to the contention of Dobrée, Nicoll, and others that Dryden's heroic dramas were elaborate tales of make-believe.[4]

[3] The author of the *Remarques* outlined a similar case against heroic drama and the society which supported it shortly afterward, in a pamphlet called *Reflexions on Marriage and the Poetick Discipline* (1673). The *Remarques* had been attacked as the writings of a rustic country parson ignorant in the ways of the Town, and he replied by upholding his dignity as "an honest Gentleman, though possible [sic] he cannot Preach so Divinly [sic] as *Maximin*." (sig. A8v) Addressing himself to a young lady contemplating a proper married state, he warned her of "*the Irreligion of the Age*," and remarked that "Your design wants none of the following Arguments to justify it, nor to keep your reason for submitting to the fantastical definitions of the self-conceited *Malmsbury* Philosopher." (sig. [A10] pp. 6-7) He explained that marriage would prevail with gallants "were they not strictly tyed up to the high Rules of their Ambition and Glory; starving their judgements, whilst they feed their pride and affection," and that it was shunned by " . . . only the Bravo's, and Furioso's of Ages, who think that the satisfying of an ungovern'd appetite, is more important, then the being kind and oblieging [sic] to common nature. . . ." (pp. 6, 23) "Nature," he emphasized, "design'd no man to that vanity, as to be taken up with the contemplation of his own endowments, like the fantastick youth, who made love to, and died for himself. . . ." (p. 139) He concluded his defense of marriage with a renewed attack upon the conception of love which had been brought to the theater "to inspire those *Bravo*'s whom they call their *Hero*'s." "They have thought fit that it should signalize it self only in prodigies of valour, and miracles of Councel: It has bestowed a sufficiency on a single Person to rout Armies, to look Kings out of their Thrones, and to make Conquests more facile then Ruine, and more easie then Traverses: It has bafled all the Stratagems of an Adversary, and wound about at pleasure the fidelity and courage of numerous Armies; all which are found but mean Exploits in the Records of their *Dryades*." (pp. 182-83)

[4] Bonamy Dobrée, *Restoration Tragedy* (Oxford, 1929), p. 28; Allardyce Nicoll, *Restoration Drama* (Cambridge, 1955), p. 88. See also for similar views, Clifford Leech, "Restoration Tragedy: A Reconsideration," *Durham University Journal*, XLII (1950), 114.

An even more openly libertine reading of Dryden's plays was made by Richard Leigh in *The Censure of the Rota* (Oxford, 1673). Leigh accused Dryden of borrowing "the Reason and Politicall Ornaments" of his plays "from Mr. *Hobs*," and of discovering "a Poeticall World of greater extent then the Naturall, peopled with *Atlantick* Colony's of notionall *creatures, Astrall Spirits, Ghosts, & Idols,* more various than ever the *Indians* worshipt, and *Heroes,* more lawless than their *Savages.*" (pp. 19, 13-14) He amplified these charges in an ironic indictment of the morality of *The Conquest of Granada:* "Another *Virtuoso* said he could not but take notice how ignorantly some charg'd *Almanzor* with transgressing the Rules of the *Drama,* vainly supposing that *Heroes* might be confin'd to the narrow walks of other common Mortals, not considering that those Dramatick Planets were Images of *Excentric Vertue,* which was most beautifull, when least regular: that *Almanzor* was no lesse maliciously tax'd with changing sides, then which charge what could be more unjust, if they look't on him as *Achilles* and *Rinaldos's* countryman, and born with them in that *Poeticall Free-State,* (for Poets of late have form'd *Utopia's*) where all were Monarchs (without Subjects) and all swore Alleagiance to themselves, (and therefore could be Traytors to none else) where every man might invade anothers Right, without trespassing on his owne, and make, and execute what Lawes himself would consent to, each man having the power of Life and Death so absolutely, that if he kill'd himself, he was accountable to no body for the murder; that *Almanzor* was neither Mr *Drydens* Subject, nor *Boabdelins,* but equally exempt from the Poets Rules, and the Princes Laws, and in short, if his revolting from the *Abencerrages* to the *Zegrys,* and from the *Zegrys* to the *Abencerrages* again, had not equally satisfi'd both parties, it might admit of the same defence, Mr *Drydens* Outcries, and his Tumults did, that the Poet represented Men in a *Hobbian* State of War." (pp. 2-3)[5]

The opinions expressed by these writers are not unique; there are numerous contemporary references to the moral eccentricities, if not irreligion, of Dryden's heroes. Almanzor was repeatedly accused of being a bully and a turncoat who regarded neither decency nor morals and until well after the end of the century, and especially during the religious quarrels of the eighties, his name became synonymous with Dryden's own supposed moral irresponsibility.[6] Other writers complained that the whole design of heroic tragedy was

[5] Leigh repeated these strictures in an essay written in connection with the controversy between Andrew Marvell and Samuel Parker. In *The Rehearsal Transpros'd* (1672) Marvell had written an attack upon Parker in which he had cast Parker in the role of the "Bayes" of Buckingham's play. Among the replies was Leigh's *The Transproser Rehears'd: or the Fifth Act of Mr. Bayes's Play . . .* (Oxford, 1673) in which Leigh not only defended Parker but commented upon the injustice of the analogy which Marvell had drawn between him and Bayes: "Then as to their *Symbolizing in their Humour & Expressions*, Mr. *Bays* you know, *prefers that one quality of fighting single with whole Armies*, before *all the Moral vertues put together*; and notwithstanding whatever the peaceable Morallist [Marvell] says to the contrary, allows Fortitude the Precedency of the *Red-Hatted* Virtues, & that Fortitude w[ch] consists in Conquering, not in Suffering, (for these two differ one from another more then Mr. *Bayes* his two *Cardinals* in *Hats*, from those two in *Caps*) whereas the Bishops Historian [Parker] gives the Palm to *Innocence.* . . ." (pp. 10-11) Mr. Bayes' preference for "*fighting single with whole Armies*" is a quotation from a speech by Bayes in *The Rehearsal* (IV, i); the same speech was quoted as late as 1687 by Tom Brown in *Notes upon Mr. Dryden's Poems . . . To which are Annexed some Reflections upon the Hind and Panther* (p. 22).

[6] See, *e.g.*, Edward Ravenscroft, prologue to *The Careless Lovers* (1673); *Satyr to his Muse* (1682), sig. B2v; Thomas Shipman, *Carolina: or, Loyal Poems* (1683), sig. N7v; Montague and Prior, *The Hind and the Panther Transvers'd* (1687), sig. A4v; Martin Clifford, *Notes upon Mr. Dryden's Poems* (1687), p. 6; *An Ode Occasion'd by the Death of the Queen* (1695), sig. A2; George Powell, preface to *The Fatal Discovery* (1698), sig. [A2]; *Poems on Affairs of State* (1703) [Case 211 (2)], p. 222; and *The Rebellion* (1704), pp. 82-83.

calculated to exalt libertinism and immorality at the expense of Christian virtues. A character in *The Reformation* (1673), for example, offering ironic advice to the would-be heroic playwright, noted as an "infallible" recipe for success: "in all you write reflect upon religion and the Clergy; you can't imagine how it tickles, you shall have the Gallants get those verses all by heart . . . believe me this one piece of art has set off many an indifferent Play. . . ." (IV, i, p. 48). Many years later, in *The Reasons of Mr. Bays Changing his Religion* (1688), Tom Brown suggested that for his "lawless *Maximines* of the Theatre," as well as for his libels against recognized society, Dryden should have been sent "grazing to *Malmsbury* Common, among some of Mr. *Hobbs*'s well-bred Citizens." (pp. 6, 21)[7]

The recurrent references to Hobbes in these attacks

---

[7] For similar attacks upon the immorality of the heroic hero, see John Evelyn, *The Diary*, ed. E. S. de Beer, III, 465-66; R. F., *A Letter from a Gentleman to the Honourable Ed. Howard, Esq.* (1668), p. 7; and Henry Nevil Payne, epilogue to *The Fatal Jealousie* (1673). In the preface to *The Dutch Lover* (1673) Mrs. Aphra Behn has an interesting (if flamboyant) passage which deliberately justifies the immorality which other writers had condemned. ". . . *in my judgement the increasing number of our latter Plays have not done much more towards the amending of mens Morals, or their Wit, than hath the frequent Preaching, which this last age hath been pester'd with, (indeed without all Controversie they have done less harm) nor can I once imagine what temptation any one can have to expect it from them: for, sure I am, no Play was ever writ with that design. If you consider Tragedy, you'l find their best of characters unlikely patterns for a wise man to pursue: For he that is the Knight of the Play, no sublunary feats must serve his Dulcinea; for if he can't bestrid the Moon, he'l ne'er make good his business to the end, and if he chance to be offended, he must without considering right or wrong confound all things he meets, and put you half a score likely tall fellows into each pocket; and truly if he come not something near this pitch, I think the Tragedies not worth a farthing; for Playes were certainly intended for the exercising of mens passions, not their understandings, and he is infinitely far from wise, that will bestow one moments private meditation on such things. . . .*" (sigs. A3v-[A4]) She makes essentially the same claims for comedy.

[41]

upon Dryden are significant, but can also be deceptive. The temptation to conclude, for example, that Dryden's heroic plays were either written or received as a thoroughgoing celebration of a Hobbesian code of ethics must certainly be avoided. Most of the contemporary comments on the rhymed heroic play were made by writers who wished to discredit Dryden or the genre and their judgments can hardly be accepted at face value. Louis Teeter has shown that Hobbes's particular statement of materialism was anathema during the Restoration period, and that even Charles II had to be careful in defending him.[8] The comments on Dryden's connection with Hobbesian philosophy, therefore, were probably intended to convey the stigma that was normally associated with Hobbes's name. John Aubrey stated, on the authority of "Mr. Dreydon himselfe," that Dryden "oftentimes" made use of Hobbes's "Doctrines" in his plays,[9] but as Teeter has shown Dryden almost invariably used Hobbesian ideas to characterize his stage villains; there is no instance of their use in the plays which suggests that Dryden intended to convey a commitment to Hobbesian philosophy as a whole —which is as one would expect. The most casual acquaintance with Dryden's life (or for that matter with the plays themselves) will show the improbability of his ever attempting to preach a gospel of Hobbes or of atheism.

Nevertheless, the number and extent of contemporary

[8] "The Dramatic Use of Hobbes's Political Ideas," *ELH*, III (1936), 140-69. See also John A. Winterbottom, "The Place of Hobbesian Ideas in Dryden's Tragedies," *JEGP*, LVII (1958), 665-83. Fujimura, *op.cit.*, allows too much of an influence to Hobbes. The philosophical suppositions which determined Dryden's conception of the heroic virtues and of heroic character may indeed resemble those of Hobbes, as Fujimura claims, but Dryden certainly did not carry Hobbes's premises to Hobbes's conclusions.

[9] *Aubrey's Brief Lives*, ed. Oliver Lawson Dick (London, 1958), p. 157.

comments which found some evidence of libertine beliefs in Dryden's plays cannot be ignored. At the very least the common contention of these contemporary observers that the heroic play appeared to owe much of its success to unorthodox displays of religious dialectic, and the almost universal recognition that the heroical hero was indebted to libertine models indicates a disposition in heroic dramatists to experiment with naturalistic ideas. If Dryden had designed his rhymed plays as Christian paradigms about the evil of heroic lust and the virtues of temperance, as some critics have argued,[10] there is almost no evidence which suggests that any of his contemporaries received them as such. There is abundant evidence, however, both in the writings of those who attacked and those who defended him, that his heroes were theatrically attractive by virtue of their intemperance and transcendence of normal standards of behavior.

Long after the rhymed heroic play had left the stage, Charles Gildon, in an attempt to explain Dryden's heroical heroes, remarked that "at the time when those characters were form'd, bullying was altogether the mode, off the stage, as well as upon it."[11] His suggestion has some merit. Judging by descriptions of the man about town in the early 1670's—whose "Trade is making of *Love*," whose "Talk is *Rhodomontado* and *Bounce*," and who "defies *Heaven*, worse than *Maximine*"[12]—some of Almanzor's characteristics may be far

[10] See especially John A. Winterbottom, "The Development of the Hero in Dryden's Tragedies," *JEGP*, LII (1953), 161-73; Scott C. Osborn, "Heroical Love in Dryden's Heroic Drama," *PMLA*, LXXIII, Pt. 2 (1958), 480-90; Jean Gagen, "Love and Honor in Dryden's Heroic Plays," *PMLA*, LXXVII (1962), 208-220.

[11] *The Laws of Poetry* (London, 1721), p. 350.

[12] *The Character of a Town-Gallant* (1675), sigs. Av, A2, [A4]. Similar charges were made by Samuel Vincent in *The Young Gallant's Academy* (1674).

closer to those of the gallants who viewed him from the pit than the grandeur of the heroic play would lead us to expect. Richard Leigh made this charge explicitly in his receipt for a Dryden tragedy in the *Censure of the Rota*: "It is but framing the character of a Huff of the Town, one that from breaking Glass-windows, and combating the watch, starts up an *Heroe*: him you must make very saucy to his superiours, to shew he is of the same stamp with *Achilles* and *Rinaldo*; then tame the savage with the charming sight of the *Kings Daughter* (or wife) whom this *St George* is to deliver from the *Dragon*, or greater dangers: to heighten his character the more, bring in a sheepish King with a Guard of poultrons to be kick't by him, as often he thinks fit his Miss. should be a witness of his Gallantry: if this be not enough, let him play prizes with Armies, still Tumults with one look, and raise Rebellions with another." (p. 18)

Leigh is not fair to Dryden, of course, and it would be pointless to conclude from his or similar attacks that Dryden imagined his characters wholly as glorified town gallants. Nevertheless it is worth stressing the debts that Dryden's heroes do owe to the code of conduct by which a portion of his audience lived, or seems to have affected to live. The disproportion between the gallant town ruffian and the gallant rough Almanzor is more apparent than real. In an illuminating passage of *Remarques on the Humours and Conversations of the Town*, its author notes: " . . . I have known a little Hector, more to glory in the sleights he is capable of using in picking up a Wench, and in the variety of his knowledge, than a great Captain ever did, in the stratagems and policies of War: the desire of glory and singularity is now as violent as ever, though its satisfaction is placed in such trifling and idle acquirements. . . ." (p. 128) To a certain extent, this displacement of the desire for glory and singularity is visible in Almanzor and his heroic kin. Almanzor's credentials in war are obviously excellent, but however much his martial prowess and valour are emphasized, the primary means by which he proves himself on stage is in the conduct of his love; and the physical fulfillment of his love is as much a matter of personal pride to Almanzor as it apparently was to the Town Hectors. Almanzor, to be sure, is not simply a libertine, but neither, as some critics have suggested, is he a convert to Platonism or a student in the school of temperance. On one occasion he almost takes Almahide by force and in another memorable instance he promises to pursue her and Boabdelin as a ghost:

When in your Lovers Arms you sleep at night,
I'le glide in cold betwixt, and seize my Right.
(p. 50; IV, 96)

And if he denies himself, it is as he points out, "because I dare" (p. 99; IV, 154); his constraint is more the victory than the defeat of his egoism and his pride.[13] Almanzor is perhaps more refined than the Hectors

---

[13] As one of Dryden's contemporaries remarked in 1676:

> To suffer Torments, Rigors, and Disdains,
> Raises the Merit of [the Lover's] Pains;
>   And of his Loyalty and Love
>   Assured Marks will prove:
> And how much more of torment he endures,
> His Glory he augments, and Love secures.

(Quoted in The Art of Making Love [1676], sig. E12v.) The Marquess of Halifax observed similarly that "Heroick refined Lovers place a good deal of their Pleasure in the Difficulty, both for the vanity of Conquest, and as a better earnest of their Kindness." (The Complete Works of George Savile First Marquess of Halifax, ed. Walter Raleigh [Oxford, 1912], p. 193.) In Aureng-Zebe, it is true, Morat surrenders his libertine pride to Christian exhortations and Aureng-Zebe is self-abnegating to begin with, but Aureng-Zebe marks a definite and significant departure from Dryden's previous practice. See below, Chapter IV, section i.

who watched him (though Dryden, as we shall see, stresses his roughness and eccentricity), but his "desire of glory and singularity" and the way in which he satisfied it would have been perfectly comprehensible to them.

The reason, I think, that this libertine desire for glory and singularity has often been neglected or explained away by critics of Dryden's plays is that it seems to be contradicted by other elements in Almanzor's character. Despite his protestations about being above morality, for example, his actions are ultimately compatible with it, as those of a thoroughgoing libertine like Lyndaraxa are not, and though Dryden exploits Almanzor's naturalistic drives, he seems also to emphasize the extent to which those drives can be magnanimous and admirable. To a modern reader this may appear self-contradictory if not unintelligible. But such concepts of heroism were familiar in seventeenth century libertine thought[14] and had already been impressively embodied in the drama of Pierre Corneille at the time Dryden began to write. Corneille's example is particularly important because analogies between the plays of the two men can help us to a clearer understanding of what Dryden was after.

(ii) The Cornélian hero

French dramatists, and Corneille especially, enjoyed an exceptional reputation in England during the period in which Dryden wrote his heroic plays. Performances of Corneille's plays in translation were common; during the first decade of the Restoration, Pepys saw

[14] For an excellent survey of the background of libertine thought in the Restoration period, see Dale Underwood, *Etherege and the Seventeenth-Century Comedy of Manners* (New Haven, 1957), pp. 10-40. See also Hiram Haydn, *The Counter-Renaissance* (New York, 1950), pp. 380-460, 555-618.

performances of the *Cid, Heraclius, Horace,* and *Pompey,* and he enjoyed *Heraclius,* which he records seeing three times. The English playwrights themselves frequently commented upon the vogue of translations during the late 1660's and early 1670's,[15] and the Court, fresh from its exile in Paris, looked with favor upon the fashion if it did not actually instigate it. Roger Boyle claimed that he had started writing plays in rhyme because he found that "his maj[y] Relish'd rather, the French Fassion of Playes, then the English,"[16] and several other writers specifically attributed the development of rhyme on the English stage to the practice of Corneille and other French dramatists.[17] Dryden himself was widely considered to have been indebted to France for source material. Edward Phillips noted that he "indulg'd a little too much to the French way of continual Rime and interlarding of History with ascititious Love and Honour"; and one anonymous critic charged that Dryden's plays were wholly owing to Corneille's example:

Read *Dry—ns* plays, and read *Corneille*'s too,
You'l swear the *Frenchman* speaks good *English* now.[18]

[15] See, *e.g.,* John Weston, preface to *The Amazon Queen* (1667), sig. A2; Sir William Killigrew, prologue to *The Imperial Tragedy* (1669); Edward Howard, preface to *The Womens Conquest* (1671), sig. a2v; Edward Ravenscroft, prologue to *The Citizen Turn'd Gentleman* (1672); [Joseph Arrowsmith], prologue to *The Reformation* (1673); John Wright, preface to *Thyestes,* sig. A3v; and John Crowne, preface to *Andromache* (1675), sigs. A3-A3v.

[16] *The Dramatic Works of Roger Boyle,* ed. William Smith Clark, 2 vols. (Cambridge, Mass., 1937), I, 23.

[17] In the *Theatrum Poetarum* (1675), Edward Phillips wrote that "the Imitation" of Corneille's habit of introducing love intrigues in tragedy, and of his "perpetual Colloquy in Rhime, hath of late very much corrupted our *English* stage." (Pt. 2, p. 28) See also Francis Fane, prologue to *Love in the Dark* (1675); and Thomas Shadwell, prologue to *The Squire of Alsatia* (1688).

[18] Phillips, *op.cit.,* Pt. 2, p. 108; and *The Tory-Poets* (1682), p. 6. For allusions to Dryden's alleged plagiarisms from the French,

Dryden himself frequently alludes to Corneille. He was unquestionably sympathetic to Corneille's criticism, borrowing directly from the *Discours* in *Of Dramatick Poesie* and later defending the essay against the attacks of Sir Robert Howard by appealing to Corneille, among others, as a precedent and authority.[19] In the dedication of *The Indian Emperour* (1667), he remarks that his play is *"an irregular piece if compar'd with many of* Corneilles," a comment which suggests that he looked to Corneille at the time as a standard of comparison for dramatic practice as well as theory; and this suggestion is supported by two other direct references to Corneille in the late 1660's: one in the prologue to *Secret-Love* (1668) and the other in the preface to *The Wild Gallant* (1669). Perhaps the most significant reference to Corneille occurs in the preface to *The Conquest of Granada*, where Dryden says that in founding the heroic play, Davenant *"heightn'd his Characters (as I may probably imagine) from the example of* Corneille *and some* French Poets." (sig. a2v; IV, 20)

These references prove nothing conclusively—as we have seen, for example, Dryden had reasons of his own for being receptive to the use of rhyme on stage—but

---

see R. F., *A Letter from a Gentleman to the Honourable Ed. Howard Esq.*, pp. 2-3; Ravenscroft, prologue to *The Careless Lovers* (1673); [Rochester], *Poems on Several Occasions* (Antwerpen, n.d.), p. 40; Shadwell, *The Tenth Satyr of Juvenal* (1687), sig. [A3]. In *An Account of the English Dramatick Poets* (1691), Gerard Langbaine attacked Dryden vituperatively for his borrowings and Langbaine's attributions went largely unquestioned for many decades after Dryden's death.

[19] For discussions of Dryden's specific borrowings from Corneille as well as his general debts to Corneille's criticism, see Dorothy Burrows, "The Relation of Dryden's Serious Plays and Dramatic Criticism to Contemporary French Literature" (unpublished Ph.D. dissertation, University of Illinois, 1933), pp. 37-109; and Pierre Legouis, "Corneille and Dryden as Dramatic Critics," *Seventeenth-Century Studies Presented to Sir Herbert Grierson* (Oxford, 1938), pp. 269-91.

they do suggest that Corneille might have acted as a catalyst upon Dryden and that a comparison of the two men might be useful in interpreting Dryden's plays. Whether or not Corneille actually influenced Dryden is ultimately unimportant (and I think impossible to determine as well); what is important is that their dramatic aims are analogous. To begin with, Corneille's plays, and his criticism, embody many of the ideals of dramatic structure which were already found in England and which Dryden himself had already absorbed from native sources. In the Examen of *Rodogune*, for example, Corneille speaks of the progression of acts in terms that correspond closely to those which Davenant used in the preface to *Gondibert* to describe five-act structure,[20] and elsewhere he praises the same virtues of surprise and suspense in the construction of his plays that had been commended by many Jacobean and Caroline writers. He praises actions which have "a brilliance which dazzles us with surprise"; he alludes proudly to the "very agreeable surprise" of Auguste's first summons of Cinna and Maxime in *Cinna*; he justifies the cunning introduction of the Infanta subplot in *Le Cid* (a heated point of issue with his critics); and in the first *Discours*, his discussion of unity of action provides a clear French equivalent of the Caroline delight with the progressively unraveling plot: "There should be only one complete action, which leaves the mind of the listener calm; but it can become this only by means of several other imperfect actions, which prepare for it, and keep this listener in agreeable suspense. This is what it is necessary to do at the end of every act in order to give the action continuity . . . it is necessary that every act leave an expectation of something which is due to

[20] *Oeuvres de P. Corneille*, ed. M. Ch. Marty-Lavaux, 12 vols. (Paris, 1862), IV, 421. Cf. Davenant, *Gondibert* (1651), pp. 23-24, and Chapter I, section iii above.

happen in the act which follows." (*Oeuvres*, V, 151; I, 44, 48, 99)[21]

From these traditional ideals of structure, which were paralleled in English dramatic criticism and which Dryden could thus readily appreciate, Corneille had created a distinctive kind of hero and an equally distinctive form of tragedy, and these too were readily comprehensible if not also emulated by Dryden. In a letter to Corneille from England in 1666, Saint-Evremond wrote: "I can reply to you that no reputation has ever been so well established in England and Holland as yours. The English, quite naturally disposed to esteem their own writers, forego this opinion, which is often well founded, and believe they honor Ben Jonson by calling him the Corneille of England. . . . You are the only one of our nation whose beliefs [*sentiments*] have the advantage of being close to theirs."[22] Even allowing for Saint-Evremond's marked partiality for Corneille, his letter is revealing, particularly his statement that English writers found common ground in Corneille's "*sentiments.*"

Recent studies of Corneille have shown that the *sentiment* most dominant in the action of his plays was the passion of *la gloire*. It is a difficult notion to define denotatively, since its full meaning for Corneille can only be appreciated by examining its operation in his plays. Octave Nadal, however, in an exhaustive semantic analysis of Corneille's plays, has attempted a general definition which is helpful. He sees Corneille's conception of *gloire* as embracing three distinct orders: society, power, and worth [*valeur*]. On the first level the hero seeks praise and homage; on the second he seeks to

[21] For the convenience of the reader I have translated the quotations in this chapter from the works of Corneille, Saint-Evremond, Nadal, Bénichou, and Chapelain.

[22] Quoted in *Oeuvres*, X, 499-500.

prove his superior ability in conflicts (either of war or of love); finally, on the third and most important, "he discovers another sort of satisfaction, which no longer depends on the success or failure of the enterprise, but on an absolute obedience to an inner law. This is the greatest glory; that which arouses the characteristic admiration and tragic sense of Cornélian drama."[23] Nadal points out that these interpretations of *gloire*, particularly the last, are frequently at variance with conventional morality. He finds that such traditional terms as virtue and duty, as they are used in Corneille's plays, do not refer to Christian ethics, but rather to *gloire* and *grandeur*. Thus, for example, *devoir* is used almost invariably as an expression not of moral obligations but of obligations to oneself. Corneille himself makes this point clear in his repeated rebuttals of Aristotle's conception of the ethos of the tragic hero. In the Examen of *Polyeucte* he says, "Those who wish to fix our heroes in a mediocre goodness, a limitation imposed on their virtue by some of Aristotle's interpreters, will not find this play rewarding" (*Oeuvres*, III, 479); and he makes a similar observation in the Examen of *Le Cid*. In an examination of Corneille's use of the terms *estime*, *mérite*, and *générosité*, Nadal finds a comparable stress on the expression of personal glory; and he concludes that it is essential in interpreting the ethics of Corneille's drama to avoid "confusing the Cornélian design with that of common morals, or that of religion."[24]

A similar view of Corneille's ethos is set forth by Paul Bénichou. Paying particular attention to the social and political history of the French aristocracy prior to the wars of the Fronde, he finds that Corneille's ethic of glory was a perfect expression of the ideals of the

[23] *Le sentiment de l'amour dans l'oeuvre de Pierre Corneille* (Paris, 1948), p. 307.
[24] Nadal, *op.cit.*, p. 305.

noble society of his age: "A constant movement carries
the noble man from desire to pride, from pride which
contemplates itself to pride which exhibits itself, in other
words, to glory."[25] Corneille, Bénichou points out,
enshrined this conception of man in his heroes and
villains alike, and made it an instrument of the sublimity
that was the hallmark of his plays: "The Cornélian
sublime . . . is born of a special movement by which
human impulse, neither denying nor condemning itself,
raises itself above necessity. It is a movement which
springs directly from nature, but which surpasses it,
a nature superior to simple nature: nature, by the open
advance of ambition untempered by any constraint, and
more than nature, by the power assumed by the ego in
escaping all bondage. Cornélian virtue exists at the point
where the natural cry of pride encounters the sublime
of liberty. The great soul is precisely the one in which
this encounter takes place."[26]

This is basically the conception of heroism that Dryden's contemporaries found in his plays. In the past the
principal obstruction to the suggestion that Dryden and
Corneille might be similar has been the traditional and
influential view of Corneille set forth by Lanson—a
view which saw Corneille's drama as psychologically
penetrating and morally profound, the dramatic dis-
tillation of the Cartesian celebration of the rational
will.[27] But as Nadal, Bénichou, and Jean Boorsch in his
articles on Corneille's dramaturgy,[28] have shown, such

[25] *Morales du Grand Siècle* (Paris, 1948), p. 21.

[26] *Ibid.*, p. 25.

[27] See Gustave Lanson, "Le héros cornélien et le 'généreux' selon
Descartes," *Revue d'Histoire Litteraire de la France*, I (1894), 397-
411.

[28] "Remarques Sur La Technique Dramatique De Corneille," *Yale
Romanic Studies*, XVIII (1941), 101-62, and "L'Invention Chez
Corneille, Comment Corneille Ajoute A Ses Sources," *Yale Romanic
Studies*, XXII (1943), 115-28.

an interpretation constitutes a misrepresentation of Corneille, not to mention Descartes. Corneille's drama celebrates the passion for glory, the apotheosis of individual integrity; its "morality," conventionally conceived, is adventitious at best. Thus, the contention that has plagued comparisons of Corneille and Dryden in the past, that Corneille is moral whereas Dryden is moralistic only, cannot be substantiated, any more than the view that Corneille's characters are psychologically differentiated whereas Dryden's are not, or that Corneille's heroes strive for rational self-command where Dryden's seek only material success and the gratification of passion. Passion, and particularly the passion for self-fulfillment, is the indispensable credential of the hero in the plays of both dramatists. Auguste's magnificent exclamation following his pardoning of the conspirators in *Cinna*: "*Je suis maître de moi comme de l'univers*," is ethically of a piece with Almanzor's considerably less elegant boast: "But know, that I alone am King of me."[29] The persistent charge that Dryden is materialistic whereas Corneille is spiritual confuses differences of theatrical convention with differences of morality. Dryden wrote in a theatrical tradition which accented physical action and which was placing increasing stress upon physical scenery; Corneille wrote for a theater which was evolving a stage of physical austerity, a difference which probably worked in Corneille's favor, since Dryden frequently had to compete with spectacle, whereas Corneille did not.

Another stumbling block which has long impeded comparisons of Dryden and Corneille is Corneille's apparent disparagement of love as a passion suitable to serious drama. Corneille's strictures on love are confined principally to his later criticism. One exception is a state-

[29] "I am master of myself, as of the universe," *Oeuvres*, III, 459; *The Conquest of Granada*, p. 7; IV, 43.

ment in the prefatory letter to *La Place Royale* (1637) to the effect that "the love of a gentleman should always be voluntary." (*Oeuvres*, II, 220) His most concerted criticism of love occurs during the sixties. In the first *Discours* (1660) he states that the dignity of tragedy "demands some great interest of the State, or some passion more noble and more masculine than love, such as ambition or vengeance, and seeks to cause fear of misfortunes greater than the loss of a mistress. It is appropriate to include love, because it is always very pleasant, and can serve as a foundation for these interests and for these other passions of which I speak; but love must content itself with second place in the poem and leave the first to them . . . . [Even in the *Cid*], which is undeniably more filled with love than any other play I have written, the duty of birth and the concerns of honor prevail over all the tokens of affection which love inspires . . . ." (*Oeuvres*, I, 24) In the prefatory letter of *Sertorius* (1662) he informs the readers that they will find in the play "neither the tenderness of love, nor the transports of passion," and four years later, in a letter thanking Saint-Evremond for defending *Sophonisbe*, he writes: "I have believed till now that love is too weak a passion to be dominant in an heroic play. I prefer that it serve as an ornament and not as the body of the work and that great souls should not let it act upon them unless it is compatible with more noble sensations as well." (*Oeuvres*, VI, 357; X, 498)

A number of writers have made much of these statements as evidence of an essential distinction between the drama of Corneille and that of Dryden, who obviously allows a prominent role to the passion of love in his plays.[30] As Bénichou points out, however, Cor-

[30] See Burrows, *op.cit.*, p. 188. Dowlin, *op.cit.*, p. 101, maintains that the love interest in Dryden's plays is clear evidence of his links with English Platonic drama rather than with Corneille.

neille's strictures are not as categorical as they at first appear to be. The letter to Saint-Evremond was written at a time when Racine's *Alexandre* was already threatening Corneille's popularity, and Corneille may very well have overstated his case in his effort to justify the heroic mode of his own drama in opposition to the fatalistic conception of passion incipient in Racine's.[31] Similarly, his attack on love in the first *Discours* may have been an attempt to differentiate his drama from the more *précieux* creations of his brother Thomas and of Quinault. But, in any case, his own assertion to the contrary, love conceived as an adjunct and instrument of glory is, in fact, a central element of Corneille's drama. An inherent belief of the aristocratic code of behavior was that the trial of love was a duplication of the trial of valor, and that both offered opportunity for proof of individual worth. Bénichou points out, moreover, that both the *précieux* writers and the heroic authors were really at one in this regard, despite their apparent dissimilarities. There is a difference only of degree between the problems of gallantry in the French romances and the problems which face Rodrigue in *Le Cid*: the object of both is to provide occasions for the protagonist to prove his worthiness and his ability to preserve his integrity.[32] It was against love which does not provide such opportunities—as it does not in the plays of Racine —that Corneille was really arguing.

Once these distinctions are granted, Dryden's concentration on love should no longer be thought to set his plays apart from Corneille's. There is, to be sure, an important difference of emphasis, but nevertheless the conception of love which appears in Dryden's heroic plays is far closer to Corneille's than to Racine's. The love of both Dryden's heroes and Corneille's is mo-

---

[31] Bénichou, *op.cit.*, p. 43.
[32] *Ibid.*, pp. 42, 44.

tivated primarily by an ethic of conquest. The constant protestations of Dryden's heroes that they are in the throes of passion are in fact their declarations, virtually their boasts, of the unbounded capacities of their souls. They are not statements of fatalism. Almanzor's love for Almahide, for example, is less a passion for a woman than for a possession, a personal achievement. "My Love's my Soul," he declares to Lyndaraxa when she tries to lure him from the disdainful Almahide, "and that from Fate is free: / 'Tis that unchang'd; and deathless part of me"; and when he hears the report that Almahide has been unfaithful to him, he declares in astonishment: "She must be Chaste, because she's lov'd by me." (pp. 116, 139; IV, 174, 200)

The *"sentiments"* of Dryden's and Corneille's plays, then, are fundamentally similar, and so too are their dramaturgical consequences. Both dramatists consistently place their protagonists in situations of crisis or delibera- tion, and both emphasize vitality and magnitude of character for its own sake. Corneille insists that "the struggle between nature and the passions, or between duty and love, occupies the better part of the work" (*Oeuvres*, I, 70), and he itemizes the conditions which promote and heighten such conflicts. He approves, for example, of Aristotle's preference for tragic actions in- volving persons related by birth or by interest—as when a husband is to murder his wife, a mother her infants, a brother his sister—because such actions are most calculated to promote conflicts between nature and passion: "The oppositions of natural feelings to the transports of passion, or to the severity of duty, create powerful excitement, which is received with pleasure by the audience." (*Oeuvres*, I, 65) However, he disputes Aristotle's opinion that in plots involving close relations an action in which the protagonist knows his victim, attempts to kill him, and fails, is not proper to tragedy.

He insists, on the contrary, that such an action "makes a tragedy of a genre perhaps more sublime than the three [others] which Aristotle avows." (*Oeuvres*, I, 68) He cites as support Chimène's unsuccessful pursuit of revenge upon Rodrigue, and Cinna and Emilie's unsuccessful attempt to take the life of Auguste. The result of such a preference, of course, is to place the effect of tragedy principally in the sublime excitation of scenes of deliberation and choice through which the hero, or villain, expresses his inner grandeur; and Corneille, in fact, constructs his plays in such a way as to provide a maximum stress upon such scenes. As Jean Boorsch has shown, the disposition for scenes of conflicting loyalties and passion was the essential determinant of Corneille's treatment of his sources.[33] Quite possibly, it may also have been the basis of his doctrine of *invraisemblance*; he once remarked that "great subjects, which strongly move the passions, and oppose impetuosity to the laws of duty or the bonds of blood, should always be taken beyond the bounds of the credible." (*Oeuvres*, I, 15)

Dryden indicated his interest in disputative and argumentative scenes at the beginning of his career, remarking in the dedication of *The Rival Ladies* (1664) that the scenes for which rhyme is suitable *"are those of Argumentation and Discourse, on the result of which the doing or not doing some considerable action should depend."* (sig. A4v; II, 139) Considering the exceptional emphasis upon rhyme in the formulation and development of his theory of heroic drama, Dryden's linkage of rhyme with such scenes indicates the degree to which he, like Corneille, believed that the soul of tragedy lay in situations and scenes presenting a conflict of passions and interests through which heroic grandeur could be achieved. There is no need to catalogue the

[33] "L'Invention Chez Corneille," pp. 115-28, *passim*.

appearance of such scenes in his plays; the rhymed heroic debates, which Saintsbury termed "the scenes of amatory battledore and shuttlecock," were a hallmark of Dryden's drama and appear with unfailing frequency in his plays from *The Rival Ladies* to *Aureng-Zebe*. Like Corneille also, Dryden believed in promoting such scenes by constructing plots which would present sharply delineated loyalties in perpetual conflict, a circumstance which the author of *The Reformation* (1673) noticed when he commented: "you must alwayes have two Ladies in Love with one man, or two men in love with one woman; if you make them the Father and the Son, or two Brothers, or two Friends, 'twill do the better." (IV, i, p. 48) Dryden, of course, could have found precedents for such situations in the numerous testing plots of Beaumont and Fletcher, in the plays of Caroline dramatists, in Davenant's *Siege of Rhodes,* and in the plays of Boyle. Dryden, however, like Corneille and unlike his English predecessors, concentrated on such conflicts to an extraordinary degree, "heightening" them with rhyme and contriving them so that *"on the result . . . some considerable action should depend."* It is a matter of emphasis, but an important one; he tended to make such struggles the basis of his actions, and like Corneille, he was particularly proud of his ability to "heighten" them, to raise them to a "higher pitch." (The heightening of such scenes, both in character and in verse, differentiates Dryden from Boyle.) It is possible, in fact, that Dryden's statement in the preface to *The Conquest of Granada* that the heroic playwright *"is not ty'd to a bare representation of what is true, or exceeding probable"* is, in part, the theoretical equivalent of Corneille's more subtle theatrical doctrine of *invraisemblance.*

The parallels between the concept of stage character in Corneille and Dryden are even more directly related to the ethical suppositions of *la gloire.* Corneille strove for characters that were "vigorous and animated" (*Oeuvres*, V, 12), and he considered dramatic vitality—for good or for evil—the emblem of a heroic character. In the Examen of *Polyeucte*, as we have seen, he defends the saint against Aristotle's preference for a hero of mediocre goodness, and in his first *Discours* he defends the villain: "a brilliant and elevated character, whose disposition is virtuous or criminal, according to which is proper and suitable to the person who has been introduced. Cleopatra, in *Rodogune*, is quite wicked; there is absolutely no crime which is horrible to her as long as she can conserve the throne which she prefers to all other things, so violent is her desire to rule; but all her crimes are accompanied by a greatness of soul which has something so elevated that at the same time that we detest her actions we admire the source from which they come." (*Oeuvres*, I, 32) It is on the basis of this principle that Corneille argues for his conception of the noble hero, and further, of a new kind of tragedy. In the Examen of *Nicomède*, he remarks: "My kind of hero stretches the rules of tragedy, in that he does not seek at all to arouse pity by the excess of his misfortunes; but his success has demonstrated that the steadfastness of great hearts, which excites only admiration in the soul of the spectator, is sometimes more pleasurable than the compassion which our art requires us to produce by the representation of their misfortunes. . . . In the admiration which we have for his virtue, I find a manner of purging the passions which Aristotle has not considered, and which is perhaps more certain than that which he prescribes to tragedy by means of pity and fear." (*Oeuvres*, V, 507-08) Corneille comes as close in this essay to describing the dramatic counterpart of *la gloire* as he does in any other of his critical writings.

It is likely that Dryden learned this concept of admiration from Corneille's theory and practice rather than from epic theory; but, in any case, his concept of stage character must surely have owed something to Corneille's example. We may remember that Dryden himself remarked that Davenant may have learned to heighten his characters from *"the example of Cor-neille."* Dryden was unwilling to go to the lengths Corneille did in defending the magnificent villain—he defended Maximin, the lustful tyrant in *Tyrannick Love,* for example, by claiming that *"The part of Maxi-min . . . was designed by me to set off the Character of S. Catherine"*[34]—but his interpretation of the noble hero was close to Corneille's. In the dedication to *The Con-quest of Granada,* in certain respects a more revealing document than the more pretentious preface to the play, Dryden points out that Homer and Tasso realized "that a tame Heroe who never transgresses the bounds of moral vertue, would shine but dimly in an Epick poem. the strictness of those Rules might well give precepts to the Reader, but would administer little of occasion to the writer. But a character of an excentrique vertue is the more exact Image of humane life; because he is not wholly exempted from its frailties. such a person is *Almanzor*: . . . I design'd in him a roughness of Char-acter, impatient of injuries; and a confidence of himself, almost approaching to an arrogance. but these errors are incident only to great spirits. they are moles and dimples which hinder not a face from being beautifull; though that beauty be not regular. they are of the number of those amiable imperfections which we see in Mistrisses: and which we pass over, without a strict examination,

[34] *Tyrannick Love* (1670), sig. A4v; III, 377. It is worth noting that despite Dryden's disclaimer at least one of his critics, Martin Clifford, saw no essential difference between Almanzor and Maximin. Clifford asked in *Notes Upon Mr. Dryden's Poems* (1687): "Prethee tell me true, was not this Huff-cap [Almanzor] once the Indian Emperour, and at another time did not he call himself *Maximine?*" (p. 7)

when they are accompanied with greater graces. And such, in *Almanzor*, are a frank and noble openness of Nature: an easiness to forgive his conquer'd enemies; and to protect them in distress; and above all, an inviolable faith in his affection." (sigs. *4v-a; IV, 16) Allowing for a theatrical tradition which expressed itself in considerably more robust terms than the French theater, this passage may stand as an English celebration of the Cornélian hero: Almanzor's inviolable faith in his affection is the principle of his glory. We should not be deceived by Dryden's allusions to epic heroes, nor should we be put off by his assault on the French *"point of Honour"* in the preface. As both Langbaine and Gildon noted, Dryden often denounces the French and uses them simultaneously.

Although Dryden's emphasis upon eccentricity and roughness may indeed seem remote from the characteristic urbanity of Corneille's heroes, the distinction is not crucial. English Cavalier drama had exhausted the courtly hero refined in the turns of labyrinthine manners and rich in philosophical sensibility; in order to impress the spectator with the admiration that Corneille could achieve by situation and dialectic alone, Dryden had to turn to something more startling. It is certainly possible that his portrayal of Almanzor as a natural man, irregular in his manners and violent in his passion, constituted Dryden's attempt to find a theatrical manifestation of *gloire* that would be acceptable and effective for an English audience. Moreover, the possibility seems even more likely because Dryden would not have been introducing an entirely new character to the English stage, but rather improving upon an old one. The English Herculean hero, as Waith has shown, was an obvious model. In addition, many of the protagonists in the plays of Beaumont and Fletcher—for example, Arbaces, Philaster, and especially Melantius—included eccentricity and roughness among their Protean characteristics, and it is conceivable that Dryden drew upon these examples as well for his own portraits of heroism. Beaumont and Fletcher's plays were enormously popular on the Restoration stage and Dryden may well have tried to exploit a character of proven theatrical appeal, a character, moreover, which traditionally invited the rhetorical exuberance of which Dryden was at this time so fond. But, in any event, Almanzor's huffing roughness, his moral imperfections, were neither Dryden's submission to Hobbes's view of the human predicament nor a repudiation of French point of honor, but rather a means of accommodating a Cornélian concept of *gloire* in a form that would be effective on the English stage.

Dryden's distance from Hobbes and his affinity to Corneille can be seen most clearly, perhaps, by an examination of a French treatise on the nature of glory, written probably in the early 1660's. The work, by Jean Chapelain, is entitled "Dialogue de la Gloire." The dialogue consists of a discussion among three persons. The first speaker argues that glory is at best an illusion, "a shadow," that it often encourages actions of evil, as witness Alexander's carnages, and that the principles of virtue are the only proper guides for human conduct. He states that "Glory, being something external to virtue, has nothing in common with it, and is fit merely to alter it or make it lose the greater part of its value." He adds further that *amour-propre* is the one quality in man's soul which promotes self-delusion, which disrupts the tranquillity of his soul, "which alone counterbalances all the virtuous inclinations which Nature has given him, and which is the eternal substance of the combat between Sense and Reason." He concludes that those who strive for glory in arms or in love are deluded in believing that "the incitement of Glory encourages them to work for society's good rather than for their own."[35] The second speaker concedes that *la gloire* may indeed be a delusive projection of *amour-propre*, but insists that it is a necessary one, for the "beauty of virtue," in practice, is an insufficient stimulus for human conduct. "We must not consider man as he should be, but as he is." He continues, "As the world goes, in order to preserve it one must follow the order of its disorder and accommodate oneself prudently to what one can do, if what one should do is not possible. The majority of mankind is lazy, weak, and squeamish." Aware of this universal human condition, the first sages searched for some realistic and practical means of holding man to virtuous action. "Among all means, they found none more useful than that of this self-love, of this primordial pride, upon which you have so rudely vented your spleen. They have extracted this good from this evil, and by capitalizing upon the very humour which makes people weak and presumptuous, they have carried them to actions which were vigorous and worthy of praise."[36] The third speaker, Chapelain himself, supports the second. He points out that man's infected imagination, the source itself of "this spiritual presumption which one calls pride and from which is born the Appetite for Glory," is at once man's greatest enemy and the most subtle means of his defense. "Against so powerful an enemy, who has his foot in man's breast and has established a throne in his fort, who holds even his Reason in irons, what better means is there to defend man from total oppression and enable him to act at all as he should, than to use craft and to make use of the power of his imagination in arriving at its goals by detours, since it cannot take a straight path. What better means is there

---

[35] *L'Esprit Classique et la Préciosité*, ed. J. -E. Fidao-Justiniani (Paris, 1914), pp. 156, 159-63.
[36] *Ibid.*, pp. 164-66.

for removing the obstacle which prevents man from acting virtuously than to make use of this same obstacle in making him act virtuously?" What better means than glory, for men "devour the bitter pill of Virtue when it is sweetened with the honey of Glory."[37]

It is this idea which lies at the heart of the plays of both Corneille and Dryden. Bénichou points out that in Corneille's drama true heroic pride seeks to identify its interests with those of morality, not to destroy them.[38] However fiercely the Cornélian hero may defend his own integrity, the ultimate evidence of his exaltation, the final credential of his magnanimity, is the fact that eventually his own good is not in conflict with the good of society. Corneille's theater clearly supposes that pride is compatible with heroism.

Dryden too believed—at least as a dramaturgical premise—that the exaltation of the self could lead to morally acceptable action. As he remarked in the preface to *The Conquest of Granada* he wished "*to show . . . what men of great spirits would certainly do, when they were provok'd, not what they were oblig'd to do by the strict rules of moral vertue*" (sig. [b2]; IV, 27-28), but he also believed that such actions could coincide with virtue. The ethical suppositions of Dryden's heroes are usually naturalistic, as his critics were quick to point out, but implicit in this naturalism is the almost quixotic desire to justify the natural man as a socially realizable hero. The primitivistic accretions in Dryden's plays, the disconcerting allusions to the old war of the reason and the passions are as much an expression of genuine idealism as they are of naked naturalism. The philosophical consequences of this combination may be confusing and contradictory (they were even to Dryden's contemporaries), but Corneille had indisputably demon-

[37] *Ibid.*, pp. 178-79, 185.
[38] Bénichou, *op.cit.*, pp. 28, 51.

strated the power of *la gloire* on the stage. The theatrical magnetism of exaggerated characterization, the excitement of ratiocinative debates and peripatetic actions, the glorification of individual integrity: these were the dramatic principles which Corneille had put into practice so successfully, and it is upon the foundation of such principles, translated and adapted to the English stage, that Dryden created the protagonists of his heroic drama.

CHAPTER III

The Rhymed Plays from *The Rival Ladies* to *The Conquest of Granada*

D RYDEN'S rhymed plays have usually been considered as manifestations of a single heroic formula. It is tempting but inaccurate to read Dryden's plays in this reductive fashion. The rhymed plays have similar characters, structural patterns, and themes and are certainly intelligible as a group, but they cannot be adequately explained as variations on the same static formula or as progressive steps in a teleological development. The individual plays are sufficiently different to be distinguished from one another and they often reflect significant changes in theatrical orientation. *Aureng-Zebe* especially marks a profound change of direction in Dryden's practice, even though it adheres to many of the conventions of the earlier plays.

The discussion which follows in this chapter deals with the rhymed plays from *The Rival Ladies* (1664) to *The Conquest of Granada* (1672) and is designed to survey Dryden's development of certain heroic themes and to consider their relation to themes and conventions of earlier English drama. The next chapter is concerned with *Aureng-Zebe* (1676), and briefly with *All for Love* (1678) and *Troilus and Cressida* (1679), and will be focused primarily upon the relation of these plays to the sentimental drama of the later decades of the century.

(i) The background of Jacobean and Caroline tragicomedy

As we have seen, Dryden's theory of heroic drama is largely derived from the ideals of Jacobean and Caroline tragicomedy, and many critics have recognized that the heroic plays themselves are also indebted to this tradition.[1] In subsequent sections of this chapter, I shall point out a number of specific analogues between Dryden's plays and those of his predecessors, but to appreciate the significance of these analogues, we must first have some understanding of the fundamental premises of the entire tradition of tragicomedy to which Dryden was responding.

As a form, tragicomedy is very problematic.[2] Its history on the Continent is generally dated back to Guarini's *Il Pastor Fido* (1589), and throughout Elizabethan drama there are what may be called "tragicomic effects"; but for all practical purposes, tragicomedy, as a recognizable genre, begins in England with the plays of Beaumont and Fletcher. Fletcher himself offered a definition of the genre in his preface to *The Faithful Shepherdess* (1610): "A tragie-comedie is not so called in respect of mirth and killing, but in respect it wants deaths, which is inough to make it no tragedie, yet brings some neere it, which is inough to make it no comedie . . . ."[3] The result of such a definition, in Beaumont and

---

[1] For a discussion of Dryden's critical debts to his predecessors, see above, Chapter I, sections iii and iv. Most of the important studies of his relationship to the earlier English dramatists are listed in notes 14 and 15 of the same chapter.

[2] The standard work on Renaissance tragicomedy is Marvin T. Herrick, *Tragicomedy: Its Origin and Development in Italy, France and England* (Urbana, 1955). See also Frank Ristine, *English Tragicomedy* (New York, 1910), and Madeleine Doran, *Endeavors of Art* (Madison, 1954), Chapter VIII.

[3] *The Works of Francis Beaumont and John Fletcher*, eds. Arnold Glover and A. R. Waller, 10 vols. (Cambridge, 1905-12), II, 522.

Fletcher's practice, at any rate, was to place an exceptional emphasis upon a pattern of stage action rather than upon the development of a theme. Their plays, like heroic drama, demand no single response, but a series of shifting responses to shifting relationships between characters. Incidents are arranged not to produce a moral but to precipitate episodes which will allow a maximum display of emotion and rhetoric, and their plays as wholes are organized upon principles of spatial design, rather than upon rules of cause and effect. In his preface to the Beaumont and Fletcher folio (1647), James Shirley put the matter very clearly in a passage which we have already noted: "*You may here find passions raised to that excellent pitch and by such insinuating degrees that you shall not chuse but consent & go along with them, finding your self at last grown insensibly the very same person you read, and then stand admiring the subtile Trackes of your engagement.*" (sig. A3v)[4]

Beaumont and Fletcher's *The Maid's Tragedy* (1611), though it does not "want deaths," offers a good example of these principles in practice. In addition to Aspatia, the "maid" of the title, there are three main characters in the play: Melantius, his sister, Evadne, and his friend, Amintor. Amintor had been betrothed to Aspatia, but upon command of the King, he marries Evadne. On their wedding night Evadne reveals to him that she is the King's mistress. Because of his respect for the divinity of the King, Amintor feels powerless to take revenge. Eventually, however, Melantius learns of his sister's lust from Amintor and forces her to repent and to murder the King. A new King ascends the throne

[4] For excellent discussions of the characteristics of Fletcherian drama, see Arthur Mizener, "The High Design of *A King and No King*," *MP*, XXXVIII (1940), 133-54; and Eugene Waith, *The Pattern of Tragicomedy in Beaumont and Fletcher* (New Haven, 1952).

and pardons everyone, but before the play ends there is a final set of turns and counterturns. Evadne kills herself when Amintor refuses to accept her as his wife; Aspatia, disguised as a boy, is killed by Amintor in a duel; and Amintor takes his own life when he realizes what he has done.

The radical discontinuity of action and of characterization—Evadne is alternately portrayed as a virgin and as a whore—and the sheer variety of situations which are exploited differentiate the play from Restoration practice. The action and characterization of heroic drama are more decorous and confined. But the differences are essentially those of degree, not kind. In most respects, *The Maid's Tragedy* is a prototype of the heroic play. The basic unit of construction is the scene, and the peripatetic action is contrived, as in Dryden's plays, not to develop a character or theme, but to provide opportunities for a multiplicity of debates and declamatory displays of passion. Thus, Amintor alternately declaims on the King's divinity and upon his own cuckoldom, Evadne upon the folly of romantic love and upon her love for Amintor, Melantius upon his loss of honor and his loss of friendship. The alternations are neither psychologically nor morally plausible, but they provide the required occasions for *"argumentation and discourse."*

One scene in the play, the argument in Act III between Amintor and Melantius, is virtually indistinguishable from later heroic debates in Dryden's plays. Melantius meets Amintor, and knowing nothing of Evadne's treachery, demands that Amintor reveal why he has been looking so unhappy. To preserve his friendship Amintor tells Melantius about Evadne and the King. Melantius promptly accuses Amintor of soiling the honor of his family, draws his sword, and challenges him to a duel. Amintor refuses to fight until Melantius goads him by calling him a coward, but once Amintor is ready, Melantius relents, declaring that "The name of friend is more than family." (Glover and Waller, I, 39) In a final turn, Melantius vows to take vengeance upon the King, and Amintor again threatens to fight with him in order to defend the divinity of the King as well as his own honor. The sequence ends with Amintor and Melantius reaffirming their friendship. The pattern of this scene is a hallmark of Beaumont and Fletcher's drama and remained characteristic of English tragicomedy until the time of the Restoration.

The same pattern appears in Cavalier drama. There are less action and passion in Cavalier plays than in Fletcherian, or heroic, drama; the characters are more abstract, as well as consistent; and the plays, generally, have more of the *précieux* qualities of the French romance than either Fletcher's or Dryden's.[5] But despite these differences, Cavalier drama represents a development of the Fletcherian tradition rather than a departure from it. Cavalier playwrights simply took the Fletcherian interest in design to an extreme. Their plays became increasingly geometric in juxtapositions of scenes and characters, and increasingly stylized in rhetoric. The dramatists often referred to their plays in terms of a formal garden, especially a labyrinth,[6] and the image is revealing. The usual Caroline tragicomedy propels its hero through a maze of situations in which he is confronted by equally appealing claims, and his heroism is demonstrated not so much by the choices he makes

[5] For a thorough treatment of the development and influence of Cavalier drama, see Alfred Harbage, *Cavalier Drama* (New York, 1936).

[6] See, *e.g.*, *The Plays and Poems of William Cartwright*, ed. G. Blakemore Evans (Madison, 1951), pp. 213, 488, 512; Sir John Suckling, *Aglaura* (1638), p. 95; Sir William Habington, *The Queen of Aragon* (1640), sig. [B4].

as by his capacity to discriminate, balance, and argue over the alternatives which present themselves.

William Cartwright's *The Royal Slave* (1636), one of the greatest successes of the Caroline court stage, is a typical example. The hero, Cratander, a Persian captive, is appointed mock-ruler by the Persian King for three days, after which he is to be sacrificed to the god of the sun. He performs his office so well, however, that the god refuses to take his life, and he is saved by an eclipse of the sun. Cratander's self-conscious role allows Cartwright to subject him to a wide variety of test situations whose obvious artificiality is perfectly suited to the equally obvious contrivance of the plot. Cratander debates his way through all the tests with sententious finesse. In love he demonstrates his worth by preserving an exemplary Platonic relationship with the Persian Queen, and in his office of mock-ruler he proves his heroism by remaining true both to his own country and to Persia. At one point, for example, he has the opportunity to rebel against Persia for the benefit of his homeland. He reacts with fine discrimination:

Like to the doubtfull Needle 'twixt two Loadstones
At once inclining unto both, and neither!
Here Piety calls me, there my Justice stops me.
It is resolv'd; Faith shall consist with both;
    And aged Fame after my Death shall tell,
    Betwixt two sinnes, *Cratander* did do well.[7]

If for Justice and Piety we substitute Love and Honor, or Love and Friendship (the intellectual content, in any event, will not be affected), we have an emblem of hundreds of heroic choices in both Restoration and Cavalier drama.[8]

[7] *Plays and Poems*, ed. Evans, p. 221.
[8] For similar debates in Restoration drama, see the discussions of Dryden's plays below. One other example, among many, may be

In the early years of the Restoration, revivals of
Beaumont and Fletcher dominated the repertories of the
two theatrical companies, and Dryden himself pointed
out in *Of Dramatick Poesie* (1668) that "Their Playes
are now the most pleasant and frequent entertainments
of the Stage. . . ." (p. 49; XV, 346)[9] The plays of
Cavalier dramatists were not nearly as popular on the
Restoration stage, but tragicomedies on the Cavalier
model were written throughout the Commonwealth
period as well as in the first few years of the Restoration,
and both Davenant and Killigrew, the managers of the
two companies and the most influential theatrical figures
of the 1660's, had had extensive experience on the Caroline stage. Dryden was thus exposed, at the start of his
career, to a continuous, and living, tradition of English
tragicomedy.

(ii) *The Rival Ladies*

Strictly speaking, *The Rival Ladies* (1664) is not
Dryden's first heroic play, a distinction which belongs to
The Indian Queen (1665). The use of rhymed verse in
The Rival Ladies is intermittent and it lacks many other
features of the later plays, notably the super-hero. But
nevertheless it is a useful work with which to begin a

---

cited from Cavalier drama. In Lodowick Carlell's *Arviragus and
Philicia* (1639), the hero declaims in the following manner on the
necessity of leaving his mistress: "Necessity inforces me to leave
th' Court, or live dishonourable here; but love . . . tells mee I cannot live but here; is love and honor opposite? they are twins that in
my soule strive for preheminence, and whilst they doe so raise it
higher, honour thou hast o'recome by helpe of reason:

> Which tells me love does live, tho honor raigne,
> But he whose honor yeelds to love, his honors slaine.

(sig. B4)

[9] For confirmation of Dryden's statement, see Arthur Colby
Sprague, *Beaumont and Fletcher on the Restoration Stage* (Cambridge, Mass., 1926), pp. 3-53.

study of Dryden's heroic drama because it is probably the first serious play he wrote[10] and it is transparently derivative, thus offering an excellent source for examining his debt to his predecessors.

The extent of the debt is visible even on the title page. Dryden calls *The Rival Ladies* "A Tragi-Comedy." Without exception in his later writings he confined the term to plays that consisted of two differentiated if not distinct plots—one comic, the other heroic. This is the sole instance of his use of the term in the traditional Fletcherian sense.[11] Dryden's discussion of plot in the dedication of the play reveals a similar debt, since he speaks of structure in terms which had long been established in English criticism.[12]

The play itself betrays its Jacobean and Caroline heritage unmistakably. Its immediate stimulus was probably Sir Samuel Tuke's *The Adventures of Five Hours* (1663). Tuke's play had been spectacularly successful during the previous season and Dryden alludes to its influence in the prologue to *The Rival Ladies*. He may also have been influenced by Thomas Killigrew's *Cicilia and Clorinda* (1663; written 1649/50) and by Boyle's *The Generall*, which was first performed in London in 1664 but which may have been circulated in manuscript before then.[13] But whatever immediate

[10] For the dating of Dryden's plays and descriptions of the first editions, see Hugh Macdonald, *John Dryden, A Bibliography* (Oxford, 1939).

[11] Samuel Holt Monk makes a similar point about *The Rival Ladies* in his notes to the play in *The Works of John Dryden*, VIII, 265.

[12] See above, Chapter I, section iii.

[13] See Allison Gaw, "Tuke's *Adventures of Five Hours* in Relation to the 'Spanish Plot' and Dryden," *Publ. of the Univ. of Pennsylvania*, Series in Philology and Literature, XIV (1917), 1-61; Ned B. Allen, *The Sources of John Dryden's Comedies* (Ann Arbor, 1935), pp. 50-66; and Samuel Holt Monk in *The Works of John Dryden*, VIII, 265-67.

effect these plays may have had upon Dryden, they are significant primarily as catalysts. Like almost all early Restoration tragicomedies, these plays owe a considerable debt to Cavalier drama, and in following their lead Dryden was essentially drawing upon the earlier tradition.

The feature which immediately relates *The Rival Ladies* to this tradition is its geometric intricacy. There are six major characters, three men: Gonsalvo, Rhoderigo (his brother) and Manuel (Gonsalvo's friend); and three women: Honoria (younger sister of Manuel), Julia (elder sister of Manuel), and Angellina (sister of Rhoderigo). By the end of the play they are amicably paired off in marriage, but for most of the action their family relationships and their loves are confused or hidden. Honoria and Angellina are disguised as boys attendant upon Gonsalvo, whom they both love; Gonsalvo, in his turn, is hopelessly in love with Julia, and she loves Rhoderigo. Manuel loves Angellina. At one point in the play, when a group of the lovers are threatened with death, Manuel observes:

> Wee'r now a chain of Lovers linck'd in Death;
> *Julia* goes first, *Gonsalvo* hangs on her,
> And *Angellina* holds upon *Gonsalvo*,
> As I on *Angellina*.

Honoria promptly adds: "Nay, here's *Honoria* too." (p. 64; II, 215-16)

There are two dramaturgical consequences of such a plot. The first is the preoccupation with design for its own sake. Most of the turns and counterturns of the plot, the confrontations and juxtapositions of character, have no necessary causal connection. The organization of characters and episodes in *The Rival Ladies* is ornamental rather than casual, and in this respect the play is essentially Fletcherian, since its spectator must, in

Shirley's words, "*stand admiring the subtile Trackes of [his] engagement.*" Such admiration, indeed, seems to have been particularly important in the early Restoration theater. Pepys speaks constantly of the "design" of the plays he has seen, and like their Cavalier predecessors, the dramatists themselves frequently described their plots with analogies drawn from formal gardening or architecture. Dryden uses such analogies often.[14]

The second consequence of the plot of *The Rival Ladies*, a corollary of the first, is that Dryden exploits dialectical dilemmas, situations in which a character must either choose or strike a balance between conflicting alternatives. In one scene, for example, Julia is forced to choose between her brother and her lover. She asks that they be friends:

> *Man.*   'Tis now too late:
> I am by honour hinder'd.
> *Rod.*   I by hate.
> *Jul.* What shall I do?
> *Man.*   Leave him, and come away;
> Thy Virtue bids thee.
> *Jul.*   But Love bids me stay.
>   (p. 12; II, 156)

There are several more sophisticated arguments in the play, some in rhyme, but this one offers a simple example of the freighted debates that characterize the later plays. Like its counterpart in Cavalier plays, it is

[14] Richard Flecknoe, for example, remarked in 1664 that the design of good plays "shu'd be like a well contriv'd Garden, cast into its Walks and Counterwalks, betwixt an Alley and a Wilderness, neither too plain nor too confus'd." [*Critical Essays of the Seventeenth Century*, ed. Joel Spingarn, 3 vols. (Oxford, 1908), II, 93.] Similar analogies were made by Davenant in the preface to *Gondibert*, by Tuke in the dedication of *The Adventures of Five Hours*, by Pepys in his discussion of Boyle's *Tryphon* (see *Diary*, ed. Wheatley, VIII, 177), and by Dryden in his preface to *Oedipus* (1679).

structurally analogous to the maze or labyrinth of the formal garden: the choice Julia makes in threading through the labyrinth is not nearly as important as the labyrinthine pattern itself and the occasions it provides for debate. Julia does in fact stay, but the situation is contrived so that—with equal dialectical plausibility—she could have left. She proves her worth, in other words, not so much by choosing a single proper course as by demonstrating that she can distinguish the fine points of many proper courses. As we shall see, this is the principle which underlies the debates in Dryden's subsequent plays, debates which similarly have little substantive content, though they provide considerable opportunities for dialectical and rhetorical display.

As we have already observed in comparing Dryden's plays with Corneille's, the fondness for such display is one of the principal characteristics of Dryden's drama and one of the primary means by which he distinguished his plays from those of his contemporaries and predecessors. But it is worth repeating that the essential pattern of his *"argumentation and discourse"* was native and traditional, however much he may have magnified it in verse and whatever stimulation may have been provided by Corneille's example. The orientation towards dialectical and declamatory rhetoric is characteristic of all Fletcherian and Cavalier tragicomedy.

The dominant theme of *The Rival Ladies* is also traditional: a hero proving his worth and love by renunciation. The most heightened scenes in the play, including the one with the longest stretch of rhymed repartee (IV, i), are those in which Julia persuades Gonsalvo to prove his love by giving her up to his rival. There is a similar situation in *The Generall*,[15] but the idea had been exploited long before Boyle's play. There

[15] See *The Dramatic Works of Roger Boyle*, ed. William S. Clark, 2 vols. (Cambridge, Mass., 1939), I, 27-33.

are many scenes in Jacobean and Caroline plays in which a lover gives up his mistress, sometimes to a friend, sometimes to a rival, as a demonstration of either his honor, or his love, or both. The idea was particularly adaptable and popular in Caroline Platonic drama.[16]

Dryden's treatment of the unrequited lover, moreover, is quite different from Boyle's and looks forward to the innovations of his later plays as well as backwards to his Caroline predecessors. In *The Generall*, for example, Clorimun boasts:

I'le save my Rivall, and make her Confesse
'Tis I deserve what hee does but possesse.

Pepys records that upon hearing this speech, Sir Charles Sedley remarked: "Why, what, pox, would he have him have more, or what is there more to be had of a woman than the possessing her?"[17] Dryden would certainly have agreed with Sedley, and even in *The Rival Ladies* he reveals his naturalistic disposition. There is a

[16] There is such a scene in Beaumont and Fletcher's *The Mad Lover* (v, i) and in Thomas Killigrew's *Claracilla* (iii, i). In another of Killigrew's plays, *The Prisoners* (1641), one of the characters is overjoyed when the heroine tells him that she knows he loves her but that she wishes him to help her woo his rival. He exclaims: ". . . to finde to have a friends place / In your thoughts . . . And that you know I love, / And not tell it, is a joy beyond / All but what your love brings . . . Thus I have gain'd / All my ends in love by having no unworthy one's / Upon her." (sig. Cv) The theme occurs frequently in Davenant's plays. One of the heroes of *The Siege* offers to give up his love to his rival, although he eventually keeps her; in *The Fair Favorite* the Queen insists that since "True love, admits no jealousie," she will woo her rival in behalf of the King; and in the second part of *The Siege of Rhodes* (1663), the Admiral, in love with Ianthe, resolves to be true to her, to Alphonso, and to himself "By loving that which he [Alphonso] may still enjoy." [*Works* (1673), section three, pp. 85, 106; and *The Siege of Rhodes*, Part ii (1663), p. 27, respectively] In this paradoxical form, the idea is found with tiresome frequency in all of Boyle's plays (see *Dramatic Works*, ed. Clark, i, 85-86), but he hardly deserves credit for originating it.

[17] *Diary*, ed. Wheatley, iv, 259.

particularly pointed scene, for example, in which two servants parody the Platonic pretensions of their masters (p. 8; II, 152), and throughout the play Dryden works hard to give the dilemmas of Julia and Gonsalvo heroic stature. Julia, for example, is in love with a man who comes close to being the villain of the play, a man who is a far cry from the virtuous heroes of Boyle's plays, and a man certainly unworthy of comparison to Gonsalvo. But at every point Julia remains heroically true to her passion. In a speech which resembles Almanzor's rejection of Lyndaraxa, she states proudly:

> Yet Passion never can be plac'd so ill,
> But that to change it is the greater Crime:
> Inconstancy is such a Guilt, as makes
> That very Love suspected which it brings.
>
> (p. 63; II, 214)

Gonsalvo represents a similar (though less consistent) advance toward the heroism of the later plays. By his willingness to give up Julia he admittedly, in his own words, feeds his "Virtue" but to starve his "Joy" (p. 36; II, 182), but he is hardly happy about it as are so many of Boyle's protagonists. Like Julia, he has a strong sense of self-esteem, and the persistence of his love in the face of continued rebuffs is, at least formally, a parallel to her heroic constancy in the face of rebuffs from her own lover. Dryden points out on several occasions that his passion is noble and capacious; and he is certainly meant to demonstrate what one character calls "the Pride of Noble minds." (p. 67; II, 219)

These advances, however, should not be exaggerated. Julia and Gonsalvo are only faint anticipations of their heroic successors, and Dryden's attempts to magnify their stature are not always integrated or consistent. Gonsalvo especially is placed in the awkward position of self-consciously posing libertine alternatives to his

professedly Platonic intentions.[18] The Cavalier theme
of the unrequited lover, in isolation, is obviously in-
tractable material for libertine heroism and not until
he wrote *The Indian Queen* did Dryden find a convincing way to use it. *The Rival Ladies* is thus
essentially a traditional play, and as such it confirms the
importance of native influences in Dryden's career.

(iii) *The Indian Queen*

The Indian Queen (1665) does not depart from the
structural principles that are evident in *The Rival
Ladies*. It has the same emphasis upon design, the same
geometric intricacy, and the same peripatetic action.
The prison scene (IV, i) in which Traxalla and Zempoalla confront Montezuma and Orazia illustrates these
principles perfectly. Dryden rings every possible change
upon the combination of the four characters. Traxalla
tries to persuade Orazia to love him and threatens to
kill Montezuma. Zempoalla tries to persuade Montezuma to love her and threatens to kill Orazia. Montezuma and Orazia affirm their love for each other; and
Traxalla and Zempoalla are false to each other and
jealous of each other at the same time. The action is
correspondingly symmetrical and contrived. Early in
the scene Traxalla draws his dagger and holds it to

[18] Gonsalvo, for example, remarks at the close of Act II (p. 29;
II, 175):

> Against her will fair *Julia* to possess,
> Is not t'enjoy but Ravish happiness:
> Yet Women pardon force, because they find
> The Violence of Love is still most kind:
> Just like the Plots of well built Comedies,
> Which then please most, when most they do surprize:
> But yet constraint Love's noblest end destroys,
> Whose highest Joy is in anothers Joys:
> Where Passion rules, how weak does Reason prove!
> I yield my Cause, but cannot yield my Love.

Montezuma's breast, at which point the stage directions read: "*Enter* Zempoalla *hastily, and sets a Dagger to* Orazia'*s breast*"; and shortly afterwards, like dancers in a ballet, they exchange positions: "*He puts her by and steps before* Orazia, *and she runs before* Montezuma." (p. 161; II, 260-61)[19] The movement of the scene, both verbal and physical, is typical of the entire play.

The structural pattern of *The Indian Queen* is thus traditional. Its characters, however, are new, for Dryden now strives to create protagonists whose stature will justify the uninterrupted use of heroic verse and will be comparable to the splendor of the scenery. As his contemporaries were to notice, Montezuma is a prototype of his later super-heroes. Dryden emphasizes Montezuma's heroic stature, in part, by contrasting him with Acacis, who is his rival in the pursuit of Orazia. Acacis is a hero of the old Cavalier school. Captured by the Incas under Montezuma's leadership, he refuses to return to his native Mexico when Montezuma rebels against the Incas and offers him the opportunity:

> No *Mont[e]zuma*, though you change your side,
> I as a Prisoner am by Honor ty'd. . . .
> If such injustice shou'd my Honor stain,
> My aid wou'd prove my Nations loss not gain.
> (p. 143; II, 232-33)

Like Gonsalvo, moreover, Acacis loves without the possibility of reward, though unlike Gonsalvo, he shows little evidence of pride. His love for Orazia is portrayed in a stylized and sentimental fashion. At one point, for example, when he observes Orazia weeping, he assumes the conventional posture of pity and wonder that had characterized the love malady of heroes in

[19] All references to *The Indian Queen* are to the text in Sir Robert Howard, *Four New Plays* (1665).

previous tragicomedies and that was to infect so many
later English plays:

> *Acacis*, is he deaf, or waking, sleeps?
> He does not hear me, sees me not, nor moves;
> How firm his eyes are on *Orazia* fixt!
>
> (p. 149; II, 242)

He dies unrequited but triumphant in Orazia's pity for
him:

> *Orazia* weeps, and my parch't soul appears
> Refresh'd by that kinde shower of pittying tears; . . .
> —Kinde death—
> To end with pleasures all my miseries
> Shuts up your image in my closing eyes. [*Dyes.*
>
> (p. 171; II, 274)

Montezuma, on the other hand, is cut in a different
mold. Like the Cornélian hero, he feeds not on pity but
on admiration, and his principles of conduct are determined less by the requirements of his love than by
his passionate self-esteem. Early in the play Acacis
underlines the difference between them, telling Montezuma:

> Like the vast Seas, your Mind no limits knows,
> Like them lies open to each Wind that blows.
>
> (p. 142; II, 231)

Montezuma (like all of Dryden's super-heroes) is proud
of his limitless capacity for passion, and his pursuit of
love is intended primarily to provide him with occasions
to demonstrate the magnitude of his soul. During one of
his inflamed outbursts Acacis tells him: "Be temperate
friend." Montezuma replies, "You may as well advise /
That I shou'd have less love, as grow more wise" (p.
152; II, 246), and Montezuma's love for Orazia

[81]

prompts him to any act of defiance, even against her father, who is a King:

> The Gods that in my fortunes were unkinde,
> Gave me not Scepters, nor such gilded things;
> But Whilst I wanted Crowns, inlarg'd my minde
> To despise Scepters, and dispose of Kings.
>
> (p. 147; II, 239)

This speech inaugurates the theme of the "huffing hero," upon which Dryden was to rely heavily in giving his protagonists a measure of theatrical *éclat*.

Montezuma is contrasted to Acacis in another way. The latter, again like his Cavalier forbears, is a gentleman in breeding and temperament. Montezuma himself is aware of the restraint and artfulness of Acacis' behavior, and he marvels over it:

> How gentle all this Princes actions be!
> Vertue is calm in him, but rough in me.
>
> (p. 149; II, 241)

Montezuma, we learn, was bred not by art but by nature; his childhood home was the forest and he was tutored in nature's simple school by a faithful retainer, Garucca, to whom he pays tribute at the end of the play:

> I owe him all that now I am,
> He taught me first the noble thirst of fame,
> Shewd me the baseness of unmanly fear,
> Till th' unlick'd whelp I pluck'd from the rough Bear,
> And made the Ounce and Tyger give me way,
> While from their hungry jaws I snatch'd the Prey:
> 'Twas he that charg'd my young armes first with toils,
> And drest me glorious in my salvage spoils.
>
> (p. 172; II, 277)

Despite the ferocity of the description, Dryden does not intend to suggest that Montezuma has been brought up in a Hobbesian state of nature, or that his principal motivation is a Hobbesian lust for power. As in the case of Almanzor, what Dryden is really after is a novel means of displaying grandeur on stage. The literature of the mid-seventeenth century includes many primitivistic contrasts of nature and art. One of the central motifs of *Gondibert*, for example, is the myth of the Golden Age which Davenant uses to portray the hero and especially the heroine of the epic, whom he distinguishes as souls uncorrupted by the refinements and duplicity of civilization.[20] Dryden applies the ancient antithesis literally, in almost physical terms. Montezuma is represented as a man who owes nothing to society, a man whose passions can be large and unconfined precisely because they are uncorrupted, and whose roughness can be noble precisely because it is unlearned. There were precedents for such a character, as we have seen, in the early super-heroes of the English stage. Dryden himself speaks suggestively of Arbaces and Bussy D'Ambois, but there were many others, some of whom were overtly primitivistic.[21] But in any event, Monte-

[20] See, *e.g.*, *Gondibert* (1651), pp. 199, 209, 276, 280.

[21] Beaumont and Fletcher's Philaster has overt primitivistic aspirations. He laments that he had not taken "some Mountain Girl, / Beaten with Winds, chast as the hardened Rocks," who would "have born at her big breasts / [His] large course issue. This had been a life free from vexation." (*Works*, eds. Glover and Waller, I, 119) Even more analogous to Montezuma is such a character as Memnon in *The Mad Lover*. Memnon is the very type of the uncouth warrior. He is boastful and extremely proud of his lack of courtly accomplishments:

> . . . I know no Court but Marshal,
> No oylie language, but the shock of Arms,
> No dalliance but with death. . . .
> (Glover and Waller, III, 3-4)

After returning from the wars, however, he falls in love and refuses to go about winning his mistress in any but the most direct manner. He tells his followers:

[83]

zuma's primitivistic roughness, particularly in love, is insisted upon as a credential of heroism, and like Almanzor's "eccentrique virtue," is more the theatrical manifestation of a Cornélian magnanimity than of a deliberate Hobbesian philosophy of power.

The Hobbesian implications of primitivism and naturalism are illustrated in *The Indian Queen* by Zempoalla and her minion, Traxalla. Traxalla has the traditional "aspiring passion" of the old Elizabethan villain, but he frequently clothes it in a new and fashionable libertinism:

> Ye keep a prating of your points of manners,
> And fill my head with lowzie circumstances,
> Better have Ballads in't, your courtly worships. . . .
> Let me alone; for I will love her, see her,
> Talk to her, and mine own way.
> (Glover and Waller, III, 12-13)

To the princess whom he loves, he announces:

> He loves you Lady at whose feet have kneel'd
> Princes to beg their freedoms, he whose valour
> Has overrun whole Kingdoms;

and when she responds that she is not ambitious, Memnon tells her:

> Ye shall be, 'tis the Child of Glory: she that I love
> Whom my desires shall magnifie, time stories,
> And all the Empires of the Earth.
> (Glover and Waller, III, 15)

Memnon is treated largely as an object of ridicule (he resolves, for example, to present his mistress with his heart after she asks him for it in jest), but theatrical characters have a way of assuming a life of their own, and Memnon is never entirely unadmirable. By the end of the play, he is considerably refined by his experience with love. Succeeding dramatists, moreover, used the same type with more serious intent. In *Love and Honour* (1649) Davenant portrays in the soldier Prospero "a forester . . . wild as the woods" (p. 4), a character of noticeably greater stature than that of his more cultivated companions in the play; and in William Killigrew's *Ormasdes*, a play printed in 1664 and quoted by Buckingham in *The Rehearsal*, the uncouth warrior becomes a full-fledged hero.

> . . . 'tis the greatest bliss
> For man to grant himself, all he dares wish;
> For he that to himself, himself denies,
> Proves meanly wretched, to be counted wise.
>
> (p. 151; II, 244)

Traxalla, nevertheless, is a comparatively weak figure, created primarily, one may guess, to satisfy the demands of symmetry by providing a foil for Zempoalla and a villainous lover for Orazia. The vital center of the play's exploration of unrestrained libertine passion is Zempoalla. As a political theorist she is blasphemous, contemptuous of "dull successive Monarchs [who] mildly sway," and respectful only of power:

> 'Tis power to which the Gods their worship owe,
> Which, uncontroul'd, makes all things just below;
>
> (pp. 155, 156; II, 251, 253)

and as a lover she is cynical and lustful:

> I must pursue my love—yet love enjoy'd
> Will with esteem that caus'd it first grow less;
> But thirst and hunger fear not to be cloy'd,
> And when they be, are cur'd by their excess.
>
> (p. 155; II, 251)

In matters of honor she provides a persistent cynical counterpoint to the play's heroic voices, telling her son Acacis, for example, that

> Honor is but an itch in youthful blood,
> Of doing acts extravagantly good;
> We call that Vertue, which is only heat
> That reigns in Youth, till age findes out the cheat.
>
> (p. 155; II, 250)

But she is also heroic, the first of Dryden's experiments in heroic villainy. She is the only character in the play comparable in energy and vitality to Montezuma, and villainous as she is, she has the inner grandeur associated with heroism. She loves passionately, if not wisely, and fulfills the *sine qua non* of all of Dryden's heroic villains by dying with sententious Roman pride:

I cannot yet forget what I have been,
Wou'd you give life to her that was a Queen:
Must you then give, and must I take; there's yet
One way, that's by refusing to be great:
You bid me live—bid me be wretched too,
Think, think, what pride unthron'd must undergo: . . .
Orazia has my love, and you [Montezuma] my Throne,
And death *Acacis*—yet I need not dye,
You leave me Mistriss of my destiny;
In spight of dreams how am I pleased to see,
Heavens truth or falshood shou'd depend on me;
But I will help the Gods;
The greatest proof of courage we can give,
Is then to dye when we have power to live. [*Kills her self.*

(p. 173; II, 278-79)

Zempoalla's derivation is difficult to trace. She may be a partial reflection of the ambitious females in Corneille's later dramas, although this is more likely in the case of Lyndaraxa, who, we shall see, is motivated solely by the desire for a throne. She may also be a recollection of the dominating or unscrupulous females in Fletcherian drama: the Evadne of the early portion of *The Maid's Tragedy*, or the designing but noble Cleopatra of *The False One*. Cleopatra, in particular, is prepared to die as Zempoalla does, with "Masculine Constancy" and "greatness of . . . mind," true to the "strong Fort" of herself. (Glover and Waller, III, 365) The immediate impetus for the creation of Zempoalla, however, was probably the advent of actresses to the English stage. In the second part of *The Siege of*

[86]

Rhodes Davenant gave a prominent share of the action
to Roxolana, the termagent wife of Solyman, and he
added her role to the revision of the first part of the
play. Hester Davenport, the first Roxolana, apparently
immortalized the role—Pepys constantly referred to her
as Roxolana and missed her when she left the stage—
and thereafter a passionate, if not raging female, became a staple of the plays of Dryden and his contemporaries.

In *The Indian Queen* Dryden used this type of character to explore the evil implications of *la gloire* and to
provide yet another contrast for his hero, Montezuma.
For where Zempoalla is largely corrupted by her
naturalistic impulses, Montezuma, equally a child of
naturalism, is not. He is untainted by social and political
ambition—always the cardinal sins in Dryden's plays—
and he does not so much disparage the common code
of honor as transcend it. He is as virtuous as Acacis, but
as free as Zempoalla; and although this antithesis is not
insisted upon in the play, it is present. Indeed, despite
his apparent lawlessness and ungovernable pride, Montezuma is paradoxically depicted as a figure of magnanimous compromise, the heroic mean between the demands of an artful and controlled society, and the consequences of a grand but brutal nature in a state of war.

(iv) *The Indian Emperour*

The Indian Emperour, first performed in the spring
of 1665, is a sequel to *The Indian Queen*. Little remained from the older play for Dryden to work with
except, of course, the scenery. Dryden complained in
the "connexion" to the two plays distributed to the
audience on the first night, "The Conclusion of the
Indian Queen, (part of which Poem was writ by me)
left little matter for another Story to be built on, there
remaining but two of the considerable Characters alive,

(*viz.*) *Montezuma,* and *Orazia.*" Dryden's solution of
his dilemma was to set the action twenty years or so
after that of *The Indian Queen* and to stipulate that
Zempoalla and Traxalla, having lived in "clandestine
Marriage" before the arrival of Montezuma, left behind
them a son and two daughters, and that Orazia and
Montezuma have produced a daughter, and—of course
—two sons. The symmetry of the play is unmarred.

When the play opens, Orazia has lately died, and
Montezuma reigns as king of Mexico. The aura of his
former grandeur remains—there are frequent references
to the greatness of his soul and the breadth of his passions—and he is still capable of outbursts of primitivistic
heroic pride:

Take, gods, that Soul ye did in spight create,
And made it great to be unfortunate:
Ill Fate for me unjustly you provide,
Great Souls are Sparks of your own Heavenly Pride,
That lust of power we from your god-heads have,
You'r bound to please those Appetites you gave.
                              (p. 21; II, 351)

But as the last two lines of this speech suggest, Montezuma is not as he once was. The Montezuma of *The
Indian Queen* stood apart from society, asking nothing
from it but a recognition of his inner grandeur; the "lust
for power," conceived in social or political terms, was
the hallmark of his unscrupulous and less noble adver-
saries, Zempoalla and Traxalla. In *The Indian Emperour,* however, Montezuma's behavior is no longer
entirely noble and he is certainly no longer self-
sufficient. Dryden himself was reluctant to admit this.
In the "connexion" he refers to "the sufferings and constancy" of Montezuma in the first and fifth acts of the
play, and in the dedication he mentions his eloquence
and "simplicity." Dryden may have been trying to

[88]

capitalize on the image of the old Montezuma, but both references are nonetheless misleading. Montezuma suffers nobly, rises to heights on occasion, and indisputably dies a Roman death, but he has only the shadow of his former glory. For he is now really the slave of his passion rather than its proud possessor. He is once again in love; but his pursuit of Zempoalla's daughter, Almeria, unlike his courtship of the virtuous Orazia, is a demonstration of his weakness rather than his strength. At times he tries to believe that his bondage to the contemptuous Almeria is a proof of his nobility. When, for example, he asks his priests about the future and tells them that

> . . . Life and Death are things indifferent,
> Each to be chose as either brings content;
> My motive from a Nobler cause does spring,
> Love rules my heart, and is your Monarchs King;
> (p. 14; II, 342)

the words are hollow, and he knows it. Later in the play, badgered by Almeria to kill his prisoner, Cortez, he consents to give such "Fatal proof how well I Love," but two days must pass before he does so:

> In that small time, I shall the Conquest gain
> Of these few Sparks of Vertue which remain:
> Then all who shall my head-long passion see,
> Shall curse my Crimes, and yet shall pity me.
> (pp. 36-37; II, 370)

The successors to this Montezuma are Boabdelin and the emperor in *Aureng-Zebe*, not Almanzor.

The real hero of the play is Cortez, the leader of the conquering Spaniards. A visitor from the civilized world of corruption and sophistication, he does not have Montezuma's pristine simplicity, although he appreciates

[89]

it. Mexico, he tells his follower, Vasquez, appears savage
only to the jaded Spaniard:

> Wild and untaught are Terms which we alone
> Invent, for fashions differing from our own:
> For all their Customs are by Nature [wrought],
> But we, by Art, unteach what Nature taught.
>
> (p. 1; II, 325)

But although he lacks the roughness of the super-hero,
he comes as close as a mortal can to heroic perfection. He is a bold and proud warrior, alert to the demands of honor and self-esteem; and he is an ardent
lover. Montezuma's daughter, Cydaria, points out his
particular heroic distinction: an honor in which "bound-
less power dwells in a will confin'd." (p. 22; II, 352)
Cortez's courtship of Cydaria is played off almost point
for point against Montezuma's infatuation with Almeria.
Every choice which Montezuma makes between his love
and his obligations to himself and to his country is re-
solved at a sacrifice of personal integrity; every decision
which Cortez makes demonstrates his worthiness. The
semantics of love and honor are not always lucid or consistent in any of Dryden's plays, but the intentions of
the debates as wholes are usually clear. Whether Cortez,
in a given ratiocinative exchange, chooses honor or love
is immaterial—in either case, his integrity is augmented,
not diminished. Early in the play, Cydaria accuses him
of not loving her and asks, "What is this Honour that
does Love controul?" and Cortez replies, "A raging fit
of Vertue in the Soul; / A painful burden which great
minds must bear. . . ." Under continued sentimental
pressure from Cydaria, however, Cortez conquers his
noble rage:

> No more, your kindness wounds me to the death,
> Honour be gone, what art thou but a breath!

I'le live, proud of my infamy and shame,
Grac'd with no Triumph but a Lovers name;
Men can but say Love did his reason blind,
And Love's the noblest frailty of the mind.
(pp. 18-19; II, 347-348)

The difference between this speech and Montezuma's comparable reference to the frailty of his "head-long passion" is that Montezuma is appealing to pity, Cortez to admiration.[22] For as Cortez had already told Cydaria, the Spaniard's "greatest Honour is in loving well" (p. 22; II, 352); and thus, by the peculiar alchemy of Dryden's early plays, when Cortez apparently cedes his honor to his love, he is in fact augmenting it. The crux is not in loving, but in loving well.

Dryden italicizes this point in the exemplum he provides of the rivalry of Montezuma's sons, Guyomar and Odmar, for the hand of Alibech, the second daughter of Zempoalla. Guyomar and Odmar disclose their passion for Alibech early in the play and ask her to choose one of them. She responds by setting an examination for them:

The choice is made, for I must both refuse.
For to my self I owe this due regard
Not to make love my gift, but my reward,
Time best will show whose services will last.
(p. 7; II, 333)

Later she reveals that in her heart she already has a decided preference:

One I in secret Love, the other Loath;
But where I hate, my hate I will not show,
And he I Love, my Love shall never know;
True worth shall gain me, that it may be [said],

---

[22] For a discussion of the importance of this distinction in the overall development of Dryden's plays, see Chapter IV.

Desert, not fancy, once a Woman led.

(p. 20; II, 348)

For part of the play, Guyomar and Odmar behave like
"the strange God-like race" of brothers of Cavalier
drama,[23] each vying with the other in acts of nobility
and self-sacrifice. But unlike the generous youths of that
previous drama, who are usually equal in accomplishment and virtue, Guyomar and Odmar are soon differentiated. The split between them is revealed in one
of the earliest tests which they encounter. Both Montezuma and Alibech are in danger, and the brothers must
decide whom to rescue. Odmar declares, "I'le follow
Love," as he runs off to protect Alibech, while Guyomar
proclaims, "I'le follow Piety," as he fights to protect
his father. (p. 22; II, 351) Thereafter they represent,
schematically, an antithesis between love and duty,
Odmar insisting that his deference to the wishes of his
mistress is proof of his love, Guyomar contending that
his filial piety is a demonstration of his worthiness to
love. Guyomar, of course, is eventually vindicated. His
supreme test occurs when Alibech requires him to betray
his father and country in what she feels is their own
interest. Guyomar refuses, exclaiming:

All I have done by one foul act deface,
And yield my right to you by turning base?
What more could *Odmar* wish that I should do,
To lose your Love, than you perswade me to?

Alibech reproaches him:

In all debates you plainly let me see
You love your Vertue best, but *Odmar* me;

(p. 42; II, 376-77)

but Guyomar remains firm. Odmar, on the other hand,

[23] See Lodowick Carlell, *The Passionate Lovers*, Part I (1655),
p. 79.

speedily accedes to Alibech's request, and the moment he has done so, Alibech realizes her own error and Guyomar's superior worth. Shortly afterwards she rejects Odmar, who proves the justice of her judgment by rapidly traversing the road from virtue to villainy:

> —I feel a strange Temptation in my will
> To do an action, great at once and ill:
> Vertue ill treated, from my Soul is fled;
> I by Revenge and Love am wholly led:
> Yet Conscience would against my rage Rebel—
> —Conscience, the foolish pride of doing well!
> Sink Empire, Father Perish, Brother Fall,
> Revenge does more than recompence you all.
>
> (p. 47; II, 382)

Despite the moral overtones of the Guyomar and Odmar episodes, they function in the drama more, I think, as a reflection of a political and social theme which Dryden seems to be developing in the play than as an elucidation of a moral distinction. It is rather perilous to discuss an over-all theme for *The Indian Emperour*. The play is such a mixture of old conventions and new characters, so crowded with incidents and turns, and so deficient in a single focal line of action that it is difficult to isolate a single theme without irresponsibly ignoring many others. And since Dryden was not always above making irrelevant scholastic distinctions for their own sake, the task is harder still. Nevertheless, there does seem to be an important, if not entirely central, image which recurs in the play and which can shed light upon it: namely, the opposition, frequently explicit, between the public and the private man.

The theme is noticeable even in *The Indian Queen*. For example, in the scene in which Traxalla and Zempoalla hold daggers at the breasts of Montezuma and

Orazia, respectively, Traxalla berates Zempoalla for her infidelity not only to him but to her country:

> The Nation in your guilty passion lost,
> To me ungrateful, to your Country most.

Zempoalla, mindful of Traxalla's own impolitic attraction to Orazia, replies by taunting him with his "publick Love" for his enemy's daughter:

> Suppose I shou'd strike [Orazia] first, wou'd it not breed
> Grief in your publick heart to see her bleed?

Traxalla then tells Zempoalla that both Orazia and Montezuma shall die, since "we have too long withstood, / By private Passions urg'd, the Publick good." (pp. 161-62; II, 260-61) In this case, of course, the use of the antithesis is ironic, and Traxalla, as Zempoalla recognizes, is condemned by the standard which he himself invokes.

In *The Indian Emperour* the opposition is used more often and for more far-reaching purposes. In our examination of the heroic ethos of Corneille's plays we observed that the greatest problem posed by the code of *gloire* was the relationship between the individual's will and his social and political obligations, between private integrity and public contract. In his later Roman plays, particularly, Corneille explored the problem in terms of the duties of kingship and the individual's relation to the state; and, as Bénichou points out, the tendency of his drama was to affirm the compatibility of inner grandeur with social and political morality. Dryden can hardly be said to have explored this problem, but it is implicit in his heroic ethos; and his treatment of the opposition of public and private virtue in *The Indian Emperour* is an attempt to come to grips with it.

For the ideal of the heroic lover which the play

presents is one who can successfully remain true to
both virtues. In a sense, all the conflicts between love
and honor in the play are metaphors for the larger
conflict between the individual's obligations to himself
and to his society. Two illustrations may help to make
this clear. In a scene which we have already discussed
in part, Alibech and Cydaria attempt to persuade Cortez
to relinquish his attack upon Mexico. Cortez maintains:

If for myself to Conquer here I came,
You might perhaps my actions justly blame:
Now I am sent, and am not to dispute
My Princes orders, but to execute.
Alib. He who his Prince so blindly does obey,
To keep his Faith his Vertue throws away.
Cort. Monarchs may erre; but should each private brest
Judge their ill Acts, they would dispute their best.

Up to this point Cortez's reasoning is perfectly orthodox
and Alibech's argument is clearly repudiated. Then,
however, Cydaria joins in:

Then all your care is for your Prince I see
Your truth to him out-weighs your love to me.
(p. 18; II, 346)

Cortez argues for the necessity of maintaining his honor,
but, as we have seen, he eventually relents, preferring
the name of a true lover to that of a true subject. There
is only one way of interpreting this *volte-face* so that it
can be intelligible in the context of the rest of the drama.
In the first place, although he is not a super-hero, Cortez
enjoys some of the iconoclastic privileges of *la gloire*;
and second, although Dryden asserts the primacy of self
in this instance, he does not endorse the extreme sub-
versive position of Alibech. Cortez is proving his ability
to love well; and as the rest of the play shows, he does

not thereby bring dishonor either to himself or to his country—quite the contrary.

That Alibech's position is not endorsed is shown when she advances a similar argument in the scene in which she tries to persuade Guyomar to betray his political faith:

When Kings grow stubborn, slothful, or unwise,
Each private man for publick good should rise.

Guyomar answers with an unequivocal repudiation:

Take heed, Fair Maid, how Monarchs you accuse:
Such reasons none but impious Rebels use:
Those who to Empire by dark paths aspire,
Still plead a call to what they most desire.
(p. 42; II, 377)

The two scenes should probably be viewed as complements which, together, are intended to resolve the heroic antinomy of the private self and the public trust. The public role of the hero, of course, had long been a traditional theme in English drama, but it seems to have acquired a particular relevance in the Restoration theater as a result of the Commonwealth experience. Both Davenant and Boyle, for example, exploited a political (or pseudo-political) atmosphere in their works. The action in *The Siege of Rhodes* and in most of Boyle's plays is deliberately constructed so that the destiny of the state hinges upon the private loves of its protagonists. With the exception of *The Rival Ladies*, all of Dryden's rhymed plays are constructed in this way and all of them make some attempt to deal with the opposition between private freedom and public responsibility: *The Indian Emperour* is unusual only in the explicitness with which the theme is explored.[24]

[24] For a detailed discussion of related themes in *The Indian Emperour*, see Michael W. Alssid, "The Perfect Conquest: A Study of Theme and Structure in Dryden's *The Indian Emperour*," *SP*, LIX (1962), 539-59.

(v) *Tyrannick Love*

Dryden's sense of spatial design is nowhere more evident than in *Tyrannick Love* (1670). He states in the preface that *"The part of* Maximin . . . *was designed by me to set off the Character of S.* Catherine," and several decades later, in the preface to his translation of Du Fresnoy's *The Art of Painting* (1695), he cites the play as an instance of the resemblance between poetry and painting: *"Du Fresnoy tells us, That the Figures of the Grouppes, must not be all on a side, that is, with their Face and Bodies all turn'd the same way; but must contrast each other by their several positions.* Thus, in a *Play,* some characters must be rais'd to oppose others; and to set them off the better; according to the old Maxim, *Contraria juxta se posita, magis elucescunt.* Thus in the *Scornfull Lady,* the Usurer is set to confront the Prodigal. Thus in *Tyrannicque Love,* the Atheist *Maximin* is oppos'd to the character of St. *Catherine."* (p. xlvii; XVII, 327-28) Dryden's use of the principle of dramatic contrast is unquestionable, although his reasoning in these passages is disingenuous, since Saint Catherine was obviously exploited to set off the character of Maximin rather than the reverse. *Tyrannick Love* is Dryden's full scale investigation of heroic villainy, and as contemporary audiences did not fail to see, Maximin holds the center of the stage.[25]

[25] Dryden tacitly admitted his interest in Maximin in the preface to the play: *"If with much pains and some success I have drawn a deformed piece, there is as much of Art, and as near an imitation of Nature in a* Lazare, *as in a* Venus," and most contemporary comments also viewed the play as essentially a showpiece for the characterization of Maximin. See, *e.g., Reflexions on Marriage and the Poetick Discipline* (1673), sig. A8v; and Martin Clifford, *Notes Upon Mr. Dryden's Poems* (1687), p. 7.

Charles E. Ward, "Massinger and Dryden," *ELH*, II (1935), 263-66, has maintained that Massinger's *The Virgin Martyr,* which was successfully revived a few months prior to the first performance

In portraying him, Dryden returned, to an extent, to the Montezuma of *The Indian Queen*. Like Montezuma's, Maximin's love is "rough"—"your passions are / So rough, as if in Love you would make War," Placidius tells him (p. 20; III, 408)—and although this roughness has none of the overtones of Montezuma's primitivistic purity, it is a barometer of Maximin's similarly great capacity for passion. As Placidius points out:

> Love various minds does variously inspire:
> He stirs in gentle Natures gentle fire;
> Like that of Incense on the Altars laid:
> But raging flames tempestuous Souls invade.
> A fire which every windy passion blows;
> With pride it mounts, and with revenge it glows.
>
> (p. 19; III, 407)

Like Montezuma also, Maximin is a law unto himself, and feeds on his colossal pride:

> I'le find that pow'r o're wills which Heav'n ne're found
> Free will's a cheat in any one but me.
>
> (p. 37; III, 430)

---

of *Tyrannick Love*, "provided the starting point" of Dryden's play. If this was the case, then the differences between the two plays are more striking and more illuminating than their similarities. The focus of Massinger's play is Dorothea, the Virgin Martyr, who sets the pietistic tone of the play and who precipitates its action. Ward claims that the love triangle of Artemia, Antonius, and Dorothea in *The Virgin Martyr* corresponds to the love triangle of Valeria, Porphyrius, and Berenice in *Tyrannick Love*, but again the difference is that Dorothea and her martyrdom are at the center of Massinger's love interest, while Berenice, a different character entirely, is at the center of Dryden's. But most important of all, there is no character in *The Virgin Martyr* who even remotely corresponds to Maximin. Ward, therefore, may be right in suggesting that the contemporary revival of Massinger's play offered a starting point for Dryden, but the starting point reveals how little Dryden's play has to do with Christian martyrdom.

There are two significant differences, however, between Maximin and Montezuma. The first is that Maximin develops to the full the rhetoric of heroic passion. The prologue to the play announces that

> . . . *our Poet in his conjuring,*
> *Allow'd his Fancy the full scope and swing.*
> *But when a Tyrant for his Theme he had,*
> *He loos'd the Reins, and bid his Muse run mad;*

and the description is accurate. The play is characterized by Dryden's fascination with the possibilities of hyperbolic rhetoric. The rant becomes Maximin's normal pattern of speech. Deprived of kings to huff and scepters to despise, Maximin, who is himself the supreme monarch of the play, has recourse to the gods. Early in the play, when his son is reported dead, he exclaims:

> Some God now, if he dares, relate what's past:
> Say but he's dead, that God shall mortal be.
> (p. 7; III, 393)

But his most extravagant rhetorical contention with the heavens is reserved for his death scene. Told that the gods have claimed his daughter, he answers:

> What had the Gods to do with me or mine?
> Did I molest your Heav'n?— . . .
> But by the Gods, (by *Maximin* I meant)
> Henceforth I and my World
> Hostility with you and yours declare,
> Look to it, Gods; for you th'Aggressors are.
> Keep you your Rain and Sun-shine in your Skies,
> And I'le keep back my flame and Sacrifice.
> Your Trade of Heav'n shall soon be at a stand,
> And all your Goods lie dead upon your hand.
> (pp. 63-64; III, 464)

He is wounded by Placidius immediately after this

speech, and he dies with a final imprecation against the gods:

Plac. Oh, I am gone!
Max.—And after thee I go,
Revenging still, and following ev'n to th'other world
     my blow: [*Stabs him again.*
And shoving back this Earth on which I sit,
I'le mount—and scatter all the Gods I hit.
                        [*Dyes.*
            (p. 65; III, 465)

The second difference between Maximin and the young Montezuma is Maximin's perversion of *gloire*. He is akin to the numerous lustful tyrants of Jacobean drama, from whom he may have been initially derived. But unlike his predecessors, unlike Valentinian, for example, he does not really depend upon his monarchical position to express his power. Valentinian's power is largely derived from an extreme perversion of the institution of absolutism; Maximin's is more the result of an extreme magnification of the self. Thus, Valentinian's boasts, as one critic has observed,[26] are a sign of weakness, a confession of the eventual powerlessness of his position, while Maximin's are the manifestation of his colossal self-confidence. This is what makes Maximin's affinity to Montezuma and Almanzor so close. Their difference, of course, rests in the purposes to which they direct their energies. Maximin has no desire to bring his ego into union with the standards of his society; he has no public conscience whatsoever. He violates rather than transcends virtue. Like Zempoalla and Traxalla, he is an apologist for the most unrestrained form of libertinism. When St. Catherine rebukes him for his promiscuity, he replies:

[26] Louis Teeter, "Political Themes in Restoration Tragedy," pp. 45-46.

[100]

If to new persons I my Love apply,
The Stars and Nature are in fault, not I:
My Loves are like my old Praetorian Bands,
Whose Arbitrary pow'r their Prince commands:
I can no more make passion come or go,
Than you can bid your *Nilus* ebb or flow.
'Tis lawless, and will love, and where it list:
And that's no sin which no man can resist. . . .

(p. 38; III, 433)

Later, after he has given orders for St. Catherine's execution, he tries to exalt this libertine code into a positive form of heroism:

How hard it is this Beauty to forget!
My stormy rage has only shook my will:
She crept down lower, but she sticks there still.
Fool that I am to struggle thus with Love!
Why should I that which pleases me remove?
True, she should dye were she concern'd alone;
But I love, not for her sake, but my own.
Our Gods are Gods 'cause they have pow'r and will;
Who can do all things, can do nothing ill.
Ill is Rebellion 'gainst some higher pow'r:
The World may sin, but not its Emperour.
My Empress then shall dye, my Princess live;
If this be ill, I do my self forgive.

(p. 57; III, 456)

Maximin's tragedy, if such it can be called, is that the love which he imagines as the ultimate exhibition of his egoistic power actually represents his self-betrayal. Maximin is an aging monarch, captured by his desires, the slave rather than the ruler of his passions:

Old as I am, in pleasures I will try
To waste an Empire yet before I dye:
Since life is fugitive, and will not stay,

[101]

I'le make it fly more pleasantly away.
                              (p. 46; III, 443)

The problem is not one of simple self-control, still less of Christian temperance—the loves of Almanzor and of Montezuma in his prime are both sensual and violent—but rather one of his heroic integrity. Though, in part, a demonstration of his capacity for passion, Maximin's love for St. Catherine is basically a weakness of old age, the testimony of the decline rather than the triumph of his self. No matter how passionate Montezuma and Almanzor become, they are always responsible to an image of themselves which is sustained by the publicly oriented approval of their mistresses; and their constancy to this resultant image becomes the means by which they can achieve the conflation of private and public responsibilities which is the indispensable credential of heroism. Maximin has no such image and no such constancy. He can be constant to nothing, because, if we may paraphrase Bishop Burnet's words on Buckingham, he has not been constant to himself. The distinction may be tenuous, perhaps even sophistic, but it was real to Dryden. Both Maximin and Almanzor are admirable; both are above the law. But Almanzor is on its good side; Maximin is not.

As a consequence of the stage power of Maximin's personality, the martyrdom of St. Catherine inevitably had to be secondary—a baroque backdrop to an altogether different kind of passion. In any case, religious martyrdom was hardly a theme calculated to appeal to Dryden. In *Polyeucte* Corneille had successfully transformed religious zeal into a vehicle for *gloire*; but Dryden would probably have been unable to follow his example, even if he had wished to. When Maximin first hears of St. Catherine, he remarks that "Zeal is the pious madness of the mind" (p. 6; III, 391), and

this was a position from which Dryden and his genera-
tion, with the turmoil of the Commonwealth period
still fresh in their minds, never receded. But there is a
form of martyrdom represented in *Tyrannick Love,* a
form already hallowed in the English theater, and this
is the martyrdom of love and honor. Both Valeria and
Berenice are martyrs in this cause, and Dryden treats
them more seriously than he does St. Catherine.

Valeria is a descendant of the self-sacrificing lovers
of Cavalier drama. Maximin orders Porphyrius to
marry her, but Porphyrius, who prefers Berenice, refuses. Although Valeria still loves him, she resolves
in traditional fashion:

> I'le show that I deserve him more than she.
> And if at last he does ingrateful prove,
> My constancy it self rewards my Love.
>
> (p. 25; III, 415-16)

Her greatest proof of merit occurs in a scene in which
she and Porphyrius vie with one another over taking
the blame for disobeying Maximin's orders. Porphyrius,
at first, not understanding that she is trying to protect
him, claims that he, not she, refused to love. Valeria
answers heatedly:

> Thus rather than endure the little shame
> To be refus'd, you blast a Virgins name.
> You to refuse, and I to be deny'd!
> Learn more discretion, or be taught less pride;

to which Porphyrius responds:

> O Heav'n, in what a Labyrinth am I led!
> I could get out, but she detains the thred!
> Now I must wander on, till I can see,
> Whether her pity or revenge it be!
>
> (p. 36; III, 429)

[103]

The reference to the labyrinth is not coincidental, and Valeria's advice to "learn more discretion, or be taught less pride" is a perfect apothegm of Caroline manners. Eventually, Porphyrius realizes that " 'Twas all th'effect of generosity," and the scene closes to Valeria's satisfaction:

> Thus by the world my courage will be priz'd;
> Seeming to scorn, who am, alas, despis'd:
> Dying for Love's, fulfilling Honour's Laws;
> A secret Martyr while I owne no cause.
>
> (pp. 37-38; III, 429-31)

Berenice, Maximin's wife, is a similar figure. The presence of a Christian martyr in the play seems to have stimulated Dryden to exploit his *précieux* material, and Berenice, too, sacrifices herself to the code of love and honor. She loves Porphyrius, but she vows to remain true to her husband even though she despises him. She tells Porphyrius that they must not be guided by "private ends":

> We both are bound by trust, and must be true;
> I to his Bed, and to his Empire you.
>
> (p. 12; III, 399)

She cherishes this trust even after she learns of Maximin's love for St. Catherine, and when Maximin requires that she either initiate a divorce or be executed, she chooses to die rather than violate her marriage bonds:

> I hate this Tyrant, and his bed I loath;
> But, once submitting, I am ty'd to both:
> Ty'd to that Honour, which all Women owe,
> Though not their Husbands person, yet their vow.

Though he loves her and wishes her to live, Porphyrius has also to admit that

She has but done what Honour did require:
Nor can I blame that Love, which I admire.
(pp. 27-28; III, 418-19)

But death alone is not enough for Berenice's honor. Standing upon the scaffold, she notices Porphyrius, in disguise, about to murder Maximin in her defense. She immediately warns "my Lord the Emperour," thereby sacrificing both her own and her lover's life; but it is her high moment, and she utters a threnody to its glory:

In death I'le owne a Love to him so pure;
As will the test of Heav'n it self endure.
A Love so chast, as Conscience could not chide;
But cherisht it, and kept it by its side.
A love which never knew a hot desire,
But flam'd as harmless as a lambent fire.
A love which, pure from Soul to Soul might pass,
As light transmitted through a Crystal glass.
Which gave *Porphyrius* all without a sin;
Yet kept entire the Right of *Maximin*.
(pp. 59-60; III, 459)

Berenice's sentiments were probably inherited from the Platonic heroines of Cavalier drama who schooled their lovers in the catechism of the faith. But she herself is the product of an altogether different code of conduct. In an extremely legalistic form, she represents the public face of heroism, directly opposed to Maximin's perverted private one. Also, like Almahide's Platonism in *The Conquest of Granada*, hers is less a devotion to ethical or philosophical principles than a demonstration of her own integrity, an expression of her *gloire*. If she recalls any previous heroines of English drama, they are probably such figures as Evandra and Melora in Davenant's *Love and Honour* (1649), both of whom were ready to sacrifice their lives to an ideal of "love and honour," and both of whom actually lamented their lost crown of martyrdom when they were saved: "Our hope of endlesse glory now is lost." (p. 33) Berenice's Platonism is similarly aggressive, similarly an instrument of glory.

(vi) *The Conquest of Granada*

The two parts of *The Conquest of Granada*, first performed in December 1670, and early in January 1671, were Dryden's most ambitious heroic plays. Confident that he had won the battle of rhyme and that he had succeeded in perfecting a new form of tragedy, he recapitulated and brought to fulfillment all the themes with which he had experimented in his earlier plays. Almanzor so dominates *The Conquest of Granada* that we are prone to forget that he shares the stage with others: with his mistress and his rival, Almahide and Boabdelin; with Dryden's most interesting female villain, Lyndaraxa; and with the couple who are at once Cavalier and sentimental, Ozmyn and Benzayda.

Almanzor himself is a composite of Dryden's previous heroes. He resembles the young Montezuma in that his most salient characteristic, the theatrical manifestation of his inner grandeur, is the roughness of his virtue. "Roughly noble" (p. 27; IV, 70) are the words with which Almahide describes him; Abdalla remarks:

> Vast is his Courage; boundless is his mind,
> Rough as a storm, and humorous as wind;
> (p. 9; IV, 45)

and Abenamar observes:

> What in another Vanity would seem,
> Appears but noble Confidence in him.
> No haughty boasting; but a manly pride:
> A Soul too fiery, and too great to guide:

He moves excentrique, like a wandring star;
Whose Motion's just; though 'tis not regular.

(p. 58; IV, 104-05)

The cause and sanction of this eccentricity is the primitivistic purity of Almanzor's soul; like Montezuma again, he is a child of nature, uncorrupted, and responsible only to the demands of his *gloire*. He makes this clear the moment he appears on stage, when he announces to Boabdelin:

Obey'd as Soveraign by thy Subjects be,
But know, that I alone am King of me.
I am as free as Nature first made man
'Ere the base Laws of Servitude began
When wild in woods the noble Savage ran.

(p. 7; IV, 43)

True to his naturalistic origins, Almanzor acts as proud as he speaks. He is Maximin's equal in rant. He rarely huffs the gods, as Maximin does, but he has no need to. Boabdelin and the royalty of Granada are always at his disposal. There is hardly a scene in the two plays, as Dryden's contemporaries were quick to notice, in which Almanzor does not huff a king or a prince; and he cultivates the rhetoric of pride and disdain to a fine degree. "Stand off," he tells Boabdelin's guards, who are advancing to take him into custody, "I have not leisure yet to dye" (p. 8; IV, 44); and when Abdalla presumes to spare his life after a quarrel, he exclaims:

If from thy hands alone my death can be,
I am immortal; and a God, to thee.
If I would kill thee now, thy fate's so low
That I must stoop 'ere I can give the blow.
But mine is fix'd so far above thy Crown,
That all thy men

[107]

Pil'd on thy back can never pull it down.
But at my ease thy destiny I send,
By ceasing from this hour to be thy friend.
Like Heav'n I need but onely to stand still;
And, not concurring in thy life, I kill,
Thou canst no title to my duty bring:
I'm not thy Subject, and my Soul's thy king.
Farewell. When I am gone
There's not a starr of thine dare stay with thee:
I'le whistle thy tame fortune after me.
And whirl fate with me wheresoe're I fly,
As winds drive storms before 'em in the sky.

(pp. 33-34; IV, 77)

In portraying Almanzor as a lover, however, Dryden
returned to the Cavalier pattern which he had explored
in such figures as Gonsalvo and Acacis, and *The Conquest of Granada* presents us with the remarkable spectacle of the eccentric super-hero being disciplined in the
manners of a Caroline gentleman. Almanzor loves
Almahide with a passion correspondent to the vastness
of his soul:

I'm numm'd, and fix'd, and scarce my eyeballs move:
I fear it is the Lethargy of Love!
'Tis he; I feel him now in every part:
Like a new Lord he vaunts about my Heart,
Surveys in state each corner of my Brest,
While poor fierce I, that was, am dispossest.
I'm bound; but I will rowze my rage again:
And, though no hope of Liberty remaine,
I'll fright my Keeper when I shake my chaine.

(p. 28; IV, 71)[27]

[27] It is worth noting that Almanzor is portrayed as a complete
novice to love when the play begins, a characteristic which links
him even more clearly than Montezuma to the uncouth warriors
of the earlier drama, most of whom were ignorant in the art of
love. See also *Conquest of Granada*, p. 9; IV, 45.

But Almanzor does not shake his chain, even after Almahide reveals that she is promised to Boabdelin. Almanzor's trial by love begins immediately. "Forgive that
fury which my Soul does move," he asks her:

'Tis the Essay of an untaught first love. . . .
Retire, fair Creature, to your needful rest;
There's something noble, lab'ring in my brest:
This raging fire which through the Mass does move,
Shall purge my dross, and shall refine my Love.
(p. 31; IV, 74)

Subsequently, though she is his prisoner, he returns her
to Boabdelin, an action which he insists to Abdalla is
heroic rather than merely generous:

. . . 'tis th'excess of love, which mounts so high,
That, seen far off, it lessens to the eye.
Had I not lov'd her, and had set her free,
That, Sir, had been my generosity:
But 'tis exalted passion when I show
I dare be wretched not to make her so.
(p. 32; IV, 75)

For the remainder of both plays, Dryden contrives a
series of situations which duplicate the same predicament
and to which Almanzor reacts in essentially the same
way. Unlike his Cavalier predecessors, however, he
does not welcome his martyrdom, and, as we have seen,
he is particularly unreceptive to Almahide's suggestion
that his love for her be sustained Platonically. As Lyndaraxa points out, and she is an instructive judge in
such matters, his "Love" for Almahide "is not refin'd
to that degree." (p. 114; IV, 172) Nevertheless, for
most of the play, Almanzor has no choice but to obey
Almahide's Platonic injunctions; and as the action
progresses, he gradually, somewhat like Gonsalvo,
exalts his self-denial into a source of further heroic

[109]

pride. When Almahide promises to marry Boabdelin in order to secure Almanzor's life and freedom, Almanzor agrees to go into exile although he would rather die:

> . . . what'ere my sufferings be
> Within; I'le speak Farewell, as loud as she:
> I will not be out-done in Constancy.
> (p. 66; IV, 114)

When Almahide herself calls Almanzor back to defend Granada, he agrees without any promise of reward from her:

> I'le do't: and now I no Reward will have.
> You've given my Honour such an ample Field
> That I may dye, but that shall never yield.
> Spight of myself I'le Stay, Fight, Love, Despair;
> And I can do all this, because I dare.
> (p. 99; IV, 154)

In the scene in which Lyndaraxa attempts to seduce him, his constancy to an unrequited love reaches an apogee of heroic triumph:

> Though *Almahide*, with scorn rewards my care;
> Yet; than to change, 'tis nobler to despair.
> My Love's my Soul; and that from Fate is free:
> 'Tis that unchang'd; and deathless part of me.
> (p. 116; IV, 174)

Almanzor denies himself, as he says, "because I dare," and his restraint is the victory, not the defeat of his pride. If there are moral overtones to this victory, they are associated with the heroic mystique of the public and the private man rather than with any orthodox system of Christian ethics. Almanzor refers to himself proudly as a "private man" (p. 51; IV, 97), while Almahide, like Berenice, is always conscious of her public obligations as a wife and queen. She confesses both to herself

and to others that she loves Almanzor, and she tells
Boabdelin himself that she would be content to lead
with Almanzor "an humble life; / There is a private
greatness in his wife." But, as she also explains, "honor
ties" her; and she resolves that

> . . . my Love I will, by Vertue, square;
> My Heart's not mine; but all my Actions are.
> I'le, like *Almanzor*, act; and dare to be
> As Haughty, and as wretched too as he.
> (pp. 63, 84; IV, 110, 137)

There is comparatively little question of morality for
either Almahide or Almanzor—she is motivated by
heroic pride as surely as he is; but her own *gloire* is
couched in the metaphor of a public trust, and Almanzor's refinement in his love for her permits him to
achieve that uncompromising fusion of the public and
the private man which in these plays was perhaps the
final heroic grace beyond the reach of art.

The evil counterpart of both Almanzor and Almahide
is Lyndaraxa, who is motivated by a private libertine
creed unrestrained by public responsibility and by a lust
for public power untouched by private magnanimity.
She is a member of the triad of Dryden's *femmes fatales*
which includes also Zempoalla and Nourmahal. Like
them, she is an advocate of completely uninhibited
naturalism:

> Yes; I avowe th'ambition of my Soul,
> To be that one, to live without controul.
> (p. 17; IV, 54)

Like them also she may trace her lineage in part from
the passionate Roxolana. Lyndaraxa is the only character
in the plays that can match Almanzor in displays of
passionate grandeur. In one of her most effective scenes,

she hears the sounds of battle from within the palace
and her voice rises to them in an antiphonal chant:

> Beat faster, Drums, and mingle Deaths more thick.
> I'le to the Turrets of the Palace goe,
> And add new fire to those that fight below.
> Thence, *Hero*-like, with Torches by my side,
> (Farr be the *Omen*, though,) my Love I'le guide.
> No; like his better Fortune I'le appear:
> With open Arms, loose Vayl, and flowing Hair,
> Just flying forward from my rowling Sphere:
> My smiles shall make *Abdalla* more then Man;
> Let him look up and perish if he can.
>
> (p. 26; IV, 68)

Lyndaraxa is most remarkable, however, for her
unique immunity to love. Unlike any other major character in Dryden's heroic plays, including Zempoalla and
Nourmahal, she is completely untouched by the softer
passion. She cultivates the rival loves of Abdalla and
Abdelmelech but only for the purposes of political
power. In scene after scene she manipulates their passions, employing the full panoply of the sentiments of
heroic love solely as instruments of her power. Her
single passion, the principle of her existence, is the desire
for a throne, and she will accept in marriage only the
lover who will make her a queen. She implies to Abdalla,
whom she consistently castigates as a "private man,"
that she will give him her hand if he can successfully
usurp the throne of his brother, Boabdelin; and when
Abdalla seeks to confirm her promise by asking if she
would definitely accept his love if he were king, she
replies unequivocally:

> I wou'd accept it; and to show 'tis true;
> From any other man as soon as you.
>
> (p. 17; IV, 54)

Throughout both parts of the play she punctuates her speech with visions of the promised crown:

> No Ornaments of pow'r so please my eies
> As purple, which the blood of Princes, dies;
> (p. 96; IV, 150)

and when, at the end of the play, she has been simultaneously awarded a crown by King Ferdinand and stabbed by Abdelmelech, she dies savoring the first and last moments of her power:

> Dying, I charge Rebellion on my fate:
> Bow down ye slaves—   [*To the Moors.*
> Bow quickly down, and your Submission show.
>   [*they bow*
> I'm pleas'd to taste an Empyre 'ere I goe. [*dyes.*
> (pp. 155-56; IV, 220)

Lyndaraxa is Dryden's most thoroughly Cornélian character. Many of the heroines of Corneille's later plays are distinguished by their driving ambitions for a throne, an ambition to which they subordinate every sentiment and every natural inclination. The dramatic problem of such plays as *Sophonisbe* and *Sertorius* is *"le choix d'un époux,"* and *"amour politique"* is the principle upon which the heroines invariably make their selection. In their aspiration for the crown, they comprehend and sustain their *gloire*. Lyndaraxa is of their breed. Not even the mighty Almanzor has the power to affect her heart or obscure her purple visions.

The antitheses to Lyndaraxa are Ozmyn and Benzayda, who are creatures of the sentiments which Lyndaraxa disdains. Neither of them pretends to the eccentric heroic virtues; their principal distinction is their refinement, particularly in their love for each other. They are both supremely accomplished in following the thread of the labyrinth, both graceful dancers in the

[113]

Cavalier ballet of love and honor. They fall in love
in what Dryden increasingly regarded as an atmosphere
congenial to heroics—a prison. They are simultaneously
conquered by each other's virtue, but since their fathers
are bitter enemies, they are forced to flee Granada in
order to preserve their love. The second part of the play
opens with their capture by the Spaniards, and it is in
reference to them that Queen Isabella proclaims that

> Love's a Heroique Passion which can find
> No room in any base degenerate mind:
> It kindles all the Soul with Honours Fire,
> To make the Lover worthy his desire.
> (p. 77; IV, 128)

Ozmyn and Benzayda are given ample opportunity to
prove Isabella's contention. Shortly afterwards, Ozmyn
comes upon his father, Abenamar, about to slay Benzayda's father, Selin. Ozmyn, realizing that he is in a
"snare, in which my vertue is betray'd," pleads with
his father to spare Selin's life. When his father refuses,
he exclaims, "Then Sir, *Benzaida*'s father shall not dye."
(pp. 86-87; IV, 138-39) When Benzayda arrives with
reinforcements who attack Abenamar, Ozmyn, in a
movement reminiscent of Boyle, Tuke and the older
Caroline drama,[28] turns about, and defends his father.
The scene closes with Selin's approval of the young
lovers, but not Abenamar's. During the course of battle,
Selin again falls into the hands of Abenamar, who will
release him only if Ozmyn offers himself as a prisoner
in his stead. Ozmyn is willing, but Benzayda insists that
"This Glorious work is then reserv'd for me"; to which
Ozmyn replies:

> Your vast ambition leaves no Fame for me
> But grasps at universal Monarchy.

[28] *Cf.* Tuke, *The Adventures of Five Hours*, Act v, scene i, pp.
64-68.

Benz. Yes, *Ozmyn*, I shall still this Palm pursue;
I will not yield my Glory, ev'n to you.

(p. 110; IV, 167)

Of course they both go, and in a confrontation scene between them and their fathers they demonstrate conclusively how much they deserve each other. Abenamar is finally vanquished by Benzayda's virtue.

Ozmyn and Benzayda are in part, as Dryden makes clear in the preface to the plays, his answer to the *précieux* "patterns of exact virtue" which flourished in the French romance; and they are in part, as we have seen, the lineal descendants of the heroes and heroines of Cavalier drama. But they are also harbingers of something comparatively new in English drama: a tentative prototype of the sentimental and domestic couple who were to flood the drama of the following century. Ozmyn and Benzayda move in an atmosphere which emphasizes sentiment and pity. The hallmark of their love is mutual compassion rather than grandeur, or conquest, or even admiration. Ozmyn admits that he fell in love with Benzayda because she took "noble Pity" upon him (pp. 44, 48; IV, 90, 93) and Benzayda cites the same pity as the cause of her love:

My pity onely did his vertue aid:
'Twas pity; but 'twas of a Lovesick Maid.
His manly suffering my esteem did move;
That bred Compassion; and Compassion, Love.

(p. 54; IV, 100)

"In Love, or Pity," Benzayda later remarks, "if a Crime you find; / We two have sin'd above all humane kind." (p. 76; IV, 127)

Ozmyn and Benzayda are filled with pity not only for each other but for their parents, and the visible emblem of the domestic piety which they obey and inspire is an access of tears. After Ozmyn has rescued

Selin he kneels to ask his blessing and mercy. Selin responds:

> I'le answer you, when I can speak for tears.
> But, till I can—
> Imagine what must needs be brought to pass:
> *[Embraces him.*
> (p. 88; IV, 140)

Abenamar, too, eventually succumbs to "headlong kindness" in a scene which looks forward to the pious domesticity of the confrontation of Antony and his family in *All for Love*:

Aben. Yes; I am vanquish'd! the fierce conflict's past:
And shame it self is no[w] ore'come at last. . . .
Ozm. O Father!
Benz. —Father!
Aben. —Dare I own that name!
Speak; speak it often, to remove my shame!
> *[They all embrace him.*
O *Selin*, O my Children, let me goe!
I have more kindness then I yet can show.
For my recov'ry, I must shun your sight:
Eyes us'd to darkness, cannot bear the light.
> *[He runs in, they following him.*
> (pp. 120-21; IV, 189)

Ozmyn and Benzayda were not Dryden's first venture into sentimentality. Acacis and Valeria had exploited the emotion of pity that had always been latent in the figure of the unrequited lover (Aspatia in *The Maid's Tragedy* is an obvious example) and even Maximin had betrayed a momentary weakness to tears when he heard the sublime dialogue of Berenice and Porphyrius on the scaffold:

> From my full eyes fond tears begin to start;
> Dispatch, they practice treason on my heart.
> (p. 61; III, 460)

But in the love of Ozmyn and Benzayda such sentiments are given greater emphasis and scope; Ozmyn and Benzayda, particularly in the second part of the play, are major figures of the drama who do fulfill their loves. Moreover, the sentiments which they generate affect others in the play as well. The words "kindness" and "pity" recur frequently in the play and none of the characters (Lyndaraxa excepted) are wholly immune to tears or expressions of compassion. "Pity," as Ozmyn observes, "dwells in every Royal Brest." (p. 77; IV, 127)[29]

Scenes of sentiment and pity, of course, were hardly new to English drama, and as Arthur Sherbo has pointed out,[30] the distinguishing feature of eighteenth-century sentimental drama was the extreme emphasis which it placed upon tears and demonstrations of sympathy and pity. Judged by this standard, *The Conquest of Granada* cannot responsibly be called a sentimental drama. Its sentimentality is only incipient and the play as a whole is carefully poised between the heroic affectiveness of the older drama and the domesticity of the drama to come. However many tears Ozmyn and Benzayda inspire, they themselves fall in love through mutual admiration of their heroic worth; throughout the plays Almanzor's eccentric virtue is counterpointed to their "exact" one; and Lyndaraxa exists virtually as a demonic parody of the sentiment which surrounds her. In *The Conquest of Granada,* therefore, encroaching sentimentalism was held in check, and Dryden continued his celebration of the ethos of *gloire*—but it was the last play in which he was able to do so.

[29] Even Almanzor remarks that "Great Souls by kindness only can be tied." (p. 36; IV, 80) See also, pp. 35, 88, 102, 118, 121; IV, 79, 141, 158, 176, 179.
[30] *English Sentimental Drama* (East Lansing, 1957), pp. 1-31.

CHAPTER IV

Aureng-Zebe and Its Successors

(i) Aureng-Zebe and the Fall of Glory

*A*URENG-ZEBE gathers up many themes and characters long familiar in Dryden's rhymed plays. The Emperor is a variation upon the old Montezuma in *The Indian Emperour*, debasing himself and imperiling his kingdom by a love he cannot control. Nourmahal is a duplicate of the lustful and villainous Zempoalla, and Arimant, who sues in vain for the heroine's love, is a carbon copy of the equally unsuccessful Acacis. Indamora is a slightly weaker Almahide, and Melisinda is a considerably more pathetic Valeria. Aureng-Zebe and Morat repeat the contrast of virtue and vice embodied by Guyomar and Odmar.

But if the characters are old, the way in which they are treated is new. Dr. Johnson commented that "The personages [in *Aureng-Zebe*] are imperial; but the dialogue is often domestick, and therefore susceptible of sentiments accommodated to familiar incidents."[1] The clearest verification of his observation is to be found in the character of Melisinda. Melisinda is descended from the unrequited lovers of Dryden's earlier plays, but she also anticipates Octavia in *All for Love*. She is a wife and she cannot thrive, as her predecessors had, by meriting the love which her rival possesses. When Morat first reveals his infidelity, Melisinda *"retires, weeping, to the side of the Theatre."* (p. 45; V, 255)

[1] *Lives of the English Poets*, ed. G. B. Hill (Oxford, 1905), I, 360-61.

Afterwards she tells Morat plaintively of her love for him. Morat replies:

> You say you love me; let that love be shown.
> 'Tis in your power to make my happiness.
> *Mel.* Speak quickly: to command me is to bless.
> *Mor.* To *Indamora* you my Suit must move:
> You'll sure speak kindly of the man you love.

But Melisinda is not such stuff as the old heroines were made of, though Morat himself, of course, is hardly the hero to inspire her. She answers:

> Oh! rather let me perish by your hand,
> Than break my heart, by this unkind command . . .
> Try, if you please, my Rival's heart to win:
> I'll bear the pain, but not promote the sin.

Morat then casts her off, and she weeps again. At this point the Emperor intrudes upon them and notices her tears. Rather than have him think that her marriage has been violated and that her "Lord" is "unkind," she says:

> Believe not Rumor, but your self; and see
> The kindness 'twixt my plighted Lord and me.
>
> > [*Kissing* Morat.
>
> This is our State; thus happily we live;
> These are the quarrels which we take and give.
> I had no other way to force a Kiss. (*Aside to* Mor.)
> Forgive my last Farewell to you, and Bliss.
>
> > [*Exit.*
>
> (pp. 55-57; V, 266-68)

The sentimentality of this farewell is particularly important because the scene is not isolated, as such scenes usually were in Dryden's other plays. The domestic sentimentality with which Melisinda is portrayed pervades the entire play.

The most significant evidence of this domesticity is
the contrast between Morat and his brother, Aureng-
Zebe. With the partial exception of Guyomar in *The
Indian Emperour*, Aureng-Zebe is like no other hero in
Dryden's previous plays. He is described, in contrast to
all his brothers, as a man

> . . . by no strong passion sway'd,
> Except his Love, more temp'rate is, and weigh'd: . . .
> He sums their Virtues in himself alone,
> And adds the greatest, of a Loyal Son.
>
> (p. 4; V, 206)

The moment he appears on stage he kneels to his father
and kisses his hand, exclaiming:

> Once more 'tis given me to behold your face:
> The best of Kings and Fathers to embrace.
> Pardon my tears; 'tis joy which bids 'em flow,
> A joy which never was sincere till now.
>
> (p. 9; V, 213)

Since his love for Indamora is his one "strong passion,"
he is at first enraged to learn that his father has become
his rival, and he threatens to rebel against him to protect Indamora from imprisonment. But she chastens
him:

> Lose not the Honour you have early wonn;
> But stand the blameless pattern of a Son. . . .
> My suff'rings for you make your heart my due:
> Be worthy me, as I am worthy you.

Aureng-Zebe rises to the challenge:

> My Virtue was surpris'd into a Crime.
> Strong Virtue, like strong Nature, struggles still:
> Exerts itself, and then throws off the ill.
> I to a Son's and Lover's praise aspire:

And must fulfil the parts which both require.

> (p. 14; V, 218-19)

For the remainder of the play he does so; he refuses to cede to his father his right to Indamora's love, and at the same time he refuses to sully the "glory"—the word is his—of his name by rebelling against him.

Despite his protestations about the strength of his virtue, Aureng-Zebe is what Indamora calls him, "the blameless pattern of a Son." The enormous capacity for passion of all Dryden's previous heroes—a capacity which Aureng-Zebe is allowed to demonstrate only with the emotion of jealousy—is gone; Aureng-Zebe is a temperate man. Gone too are the roughness which characterized the earlier heroes and the rant which was the emblem of their heroic pride. Aureng-Zebe's failure to embody these qualities would not alone signify Dryden's departure from his earlier conception of heroic drama: Guyomar, for example, had been drawn on similar lines in *The Indian Emperour*. But Guyomar shared the stage with Cortez; Aureng-Zebe is the only hero of the play which bears his name. All the marks of heroic virtue which he lacks are appropriated by Morat, and in Morat the quest for personal glory which had distinguished such characters as Almanzor and Montezuma is stigmatized as unmistakable evidence of villainy. Dryden thus splits the hero, and in the process he irrevocably undermines the heroic ethos which had animated his earlier plays.

The change is discernible the moment Morat makes his first appearance. He is a soldier, proud in his power of arms, triumphant in his speech:

To me, the cries of fighting Fields are Charms:
Keen be my Sab[r]e, and of proof my Arms.
I ask no other blessing of my Stars:
No prize but Fame, nor Mistris but the Wars.

> (sig. F2; V, 243)

[121]

He also aspires to greatness:

Me-thinks all pleasure is in greatness found.
Kings, like Heav'ns Eye, should spread their beams
    around.
Pleas'd to be seen while Glory's race they run.
                              (sig. F2v; V, 243-44)

But his designs upon the state are unscrupulous; and
the maxims by which he proposes to rule are the hall-
marks of political villainy. Like his heroic forbears, he
is a child of nature, but of a nature which Dryden now
makes clear is nasty, solitary, and brutish, the reverse
of the natural paradise which nourished the virtues of
Montezuma and Almanzor. Aureng-Zebe remarks to
Morat:

When thou wert form'd, Heav'n did a Man begin;
But the brute Soul, by chance, was shuffl'd in.
In Woods and Wilds thy Monar[c]hy maintain:
Where valiant Beasts, by force and rapine, reign.
In Life's next Scene, if Transmigration be,
Some Bear or Lion is reserv'd for thee.
                              (p. 40; V, 248)[2]

But this is not the worst of the indignities which
Morat's grandeur must suffer. In what is certainly one
of the most extraordinary scenes in all of Dryden's
heroic drama, Indamora successfully persuades Morat

---

[2] Aureng-Zebe uses similar language in condemning Nourmahal
when he realizes that she is trying to seduce him:

Hence, hence, and to some barbarous Climate fly,
Which onely Brutes in humane form does yield,
And Man grows wild in Nature's common Field.
                              (pp. 51-52; V, 261)

Cf. Montezuma's account of his wild upbringing (*The Indian Queen*,
in Sir Robert Howard, *Four New Plays*, p. 172; II, 277) and Almanzor's boast of kinship with the noble savage. (*The Conquest of
Granada*, p. 7; IV, 43)

to abandon forever the corrupt code by which he lives.
Morat argues that usurpation by force eventually justifies itself:

> But who by force a Scepter does obtain,
> Shows he can govern that which he could gain.

Indamora replies that such a doctrine is an invitation
to an anarchy of power, and Morat begins his retreat:

> I without guilt, would mount the Royal Seat;
> But yet 'tis necessary to be great.
> *Ind.* All Greatness is in Virtue understood:
> 'Tis onely necessary to be good.
> Tell me, what is't at which great Spirits aim,
> What most your self desire?
> *Mor.* —Renown, and Fame,
> And Pow'r, as uncontrol'd as is my will.
> *Ind.* How you confound desires of good and ill!
> For true renown is still with Virtue joyn'd;
> But lust of Pow'r lets loose th'unbridl'd mind.
> Yours is a Soul irregularly great,
> Which wanting temper, yet abounds with heat:
> So strong, yet so unequal pulses beat.
> A Sun which does, through vapours dimnly shine:
> What pity 'tis you are not all Divine! . . .
> Dare to be great, without a guilty Crown;
> View it, and lay the bright temptation down:
> 'Tis base to seize on all, because you may;
> That's Empire, that which I can give away:
> There's joy when to wild Will you Laws prescribe,
> When you bid Fortune carry back her Bribe:
> A joy, which none but greatest minds can taste;
> A Fame, which will to endless Ages last.
> *Mor.* Renown, and Fame, in vain, I courted long;
> And still pursu'd 'em, though directed wrong. . . .
> Unjust Dominion I no more pursue;

I quit all other claims but those to you.
(pp. 68-69; V, 280-82)

Morat does not give up his claims to Indamora, even at his death, but he signifies his reclamation by renouncing his "pleasure to destroy" and by showing generous feelings towards both his brother and Indamora herself. (pp. 69-70; V, 282-83)

There are, of course, many scenes in heroic drama in which the villain converts to virtue on his deathbed. But Morat's capitulation involves far more than himself. With his fall from grandeur, and with Aureng-Zebe's corresponding rise to the virtues of love and piety, Dryden, in effect, recognized the exhaustion of the form of drama which only four years before he had acclaimed as the equal of the tragedies of the last age. *Aureng-Zebe* does not mark a total break with the earlier plays. The peripatetic stage pattern remains, as it was to remain in the drama for years to come; and though the super-hero is clearly repudiated, some of his principles survive. Both Aureng-Zebe and Indamora seek to make themselves worthy of each other, and love and honor are still the principal catchwords. The play closes, in fact, with the Emperor giving Aureng-Zebe Indamora's hand as his "just [reward] of Love and Honour." (p. 86; V, 302) But if the topics are the same—the *"mistaken Topicks of Tragedy,"* Dryden was later to call them—the purposes for which they are used have begun to change. Pity and the capacity for tears have begun to supersede the union of private and public pride as the credentials of heroism, and the focal scenes are those which occasion a display of these sentiments rather than those which demonstrate grandeur and evoke admiration.[3] The virtues which Indamora and Aureng-Zebe

---

[3] This change of focus is evident not only in the scenes and speeches that have been cited, but throughout *Aureng-Zebe*. Com-

insist upon are those of private life, and there is no corresponding emphasis upon public responsibility. Aureng-Zebe is less the best of subjects than he is the best of sons, one of the first heralds of the paragons of

---

passion is a constant touchstone of virtue in the play. During their first scene together Indamora tells Melisinda that because she is "Distress'd" herself, she "therefore can compassion take, and give," and Melisinda, in return, promises to "pay the charity" which Indamora has "lent [her] grief." (sigs. F, Fv; V, 241-42) In a later scene, when their positions seem to have been reversed, Melisinda remarks:

> Madam, the strange reverse of Fate you see:
> I piti'd you, now you may pity me.
> (p. 47; V, 256)

Indamora praises Ariment for his "generous Pity" (p. 16; V, 221) and tells Morat when she pleads for Aureng-Zebe's life:

> Had Heav'n the Crown for *Aureng-Zebe* design'd,
> Pity, for you, had pierc'd his generous mind.
> Pity does with a Noble Nature suit:
> A Brother's life had suffer'd no dispute.
> (p. 45; V, 254)

Aureng-Zebe confirms Indamora's judgment by taking pity upon Nourmahal, who he thinks is his enemy (p. 25; V, 231) and upon the Emperor, who he knows has been his rival. (p. 64; V, 277)

All the virtuous characters, moreover, demonstrate their compassion by crying. Aureng-Zebe sheds tears when he first sees his father, (p. 9; V, 213) and weeps as a means of earning Indamora's forgiveness after a quarrel. (p. 63; V, 275) Indamora kneels to Nourmahal in tears (p. 74; V, 287), and weeps at Morat's death, as she explains to the jealous Aureng-Zebe, in tribute to her own redemptive powers:

> Those tears you saw, that tenderness I show'd,
> Were just effects of grief and gratitude.
> He di'd my Convert.
> (p. 81; V, 296)

Melisinda is described as "bath'd in tears" before the audience ever sees her (sig. E4v; V, 239), and the moment she does appear, Indamora greets her as a personification of grief:

> When graceful sorrow in her pomp appears,
> Sure she is dress'd in *Melisinda*'s tears.
> (sig. F; V, 240)

[125]

filial devotion that abound in eighteenth-century plays.[4] In Morat's case even the antinomy of love and honor itself begins to be sapped at its roots, for he gives up an honor which, though corrupted, still bears the marks of the old heroic grandeur; and he gives it up *for* love. This is the first time in all of Dryden's drama that love and honor constitute a real antithesis, and the victory of love in this context spells the end of the heroic play. Two years later, Antony also gives up honor, and he does so all for love.

The subversion of the heroic ethos in *Aureng-Zebe* and the exploitation of sentiment are also reflected in the play's verse structure. Saintsbury pointed out that "There is in *Aurengzebe* a great tendency towards *enjambement*; and as soon as this tendency gets the upper hand, a recurrence to blank verse is, in English dramatic writing, tolerably certain."[5] Dryden himself

---

On one occasion Melisinda even delivers a lecture on the beneficence of tears:

> *Ind.* I'm stupifi'd with sorrow, past relief
> Of tears: parch'd up, and wither'd with my grief.
> *Mel.* Dry mourning will decays more deadly bring,
> As a North Wind burns a too forward Spring.
> Give sorrow vent, and let the sluces go.
>
> (p. 71; V, 284-85)

[4] The emphasis upon family relationships throughout *Aureng-Zebe* is notable. For the first time in Dryden's plays, family piety becomes an essential means of differentiating virtue and vice. The virtuous characters in the play are uniformly conscious of their domestic obligations. Aureng-Zebe, as we have seen, is the best of sons; Indamora promises to be the best of daughters-in-law; and Melisinda, as Dryden remarks of her in the dedication, is *"a Woman passionately loving of her husband, patient of injuries and contempt, and constant in her kindness, to the last. . . ."* (sig. a; V, 198) On the other hand, the Emperor is loyal neither to his son nor to his wife; Morat is both unconstant and brutal to his wife; and Nourmahal, who boasts that "Love sure's a name that's more Divine than Wife," (p. 41; V, 250) entertains desires that are incestuous as well as unfaithful.

[5] *Dryden* (London, 1881), p. 57.

is aware that this is happening, for he complains in the prologue to the play that he

Grows weary of his long-lov'd Mistris, Rhyme.
Passion's too fierce to be in Fetters bound,
And Nature flies him like Enchanted Ground.

In the dedication he remarks that *"If I must be con-*
demn'd to Rhyme, I should find some ease in my change
of punishment. I desire to be no longer the Sisyphus *of*
the Stage; to rowl up a Stone *with endless labour (which*
to follow the proverb, gathers no Mosse) *and which is*
perpetually falling down again." (sig. [A4]; V, 195)
Given Dryden's extraordinary stress upon rhyme in his
earlier theory and practice, these statements are important. They are not simply the expression of weariness
or impatience with the couplet itself—he continued to
use rhyme with obvious success in his poetry—but rather
a critical recognition that the purpose of serious drama
was changing and that therefore the artifice of rhyme
could no longer exercise its proper function in the
theater. Dryden's great ambition, as we have seen, was
to perfect upon the English stage a language of tragedy
that would *"confess, as well the labour as the force of*
his imagination," but the practice of such a language, as
he had repeatedly argued, was contingent upon a conception of tragedy which could justify it. Rhyme, as
Dryden himself quickly realized, had no place in the
speech of heroes whom the spectators were supposed to
sympathize with rather than admire, nor in a theater
which emphasized illusion rather than artifice. The same
principle of decorum by which Dryden justified rhyme
for the representation of grandeur and glory compelled
him to acknowledge its inappropriateness for the portrayal of sentiment and piety.

In both its form and substance, therefore, *Aureng-*
Zebe represents a turning point in Dryden's dramatic

career. The chastened versification, Morat's conversion and the repudiation of his aspirations to personal glory, Aureng-Zebe's temperance and family loyalty, Melisinda's unrelieved distress, and the general disposition of all the exemplary characters to demonstrate their virtue through tears and compassion mark Dryden's distinct departure from his earlier ideals of heroic drama and anticipate the stress upon domestic piety and compassion that characterizes his subsequent plays as well as those of his contemporaries.

(ii) *All for Love*

All for Love preserves many of the features of Dryden's rhymed plays. It is peripatetic in structure; and it purports to deal with heroic issues: Antony's love is presented, in the words of one recent critic, as "a suitable enterprise for a hero."[6] As in *Aureng-Zebe*, however, the heroism of *All for Love* is subverted at every turn by sentimental effects which emphasize not the heroic glory of love, but its domesticity and compassion. In *All for Love* Dryden develops the sentimental tendencies of his earlier plays and responds, as we shall see, to the challenge that had been offered by the passionate drama of his young and highly popular contemporaries, Lee and Otway.

Dryden gives some indication of his sentimental intentions in the preface, where he remarks that he designed the play "to work up the pity [of the original story] to a greater heighth . . . " and criticizes himself for introducing Octavia, who by "the dividing of pity" between her and Cleopatra, "like the cutting of a River into many Channels, abated the strength of the natural stream." He is even more explicit in the prologue. The author, he writes:

[6] Waith, *The Herculean Hero*, p. 200. Waith's interpretation of *All for Love* differs markedly from mine; see *ibid.*, pp. 188-200.

. . . fights this day unarm'd; without his Rhyme.
And brings a Tale which often has been told;
As sad as Dido's; *and almost as old.*
His Heroe, whom you Wits his Bully call,
Bates of his mettle; and scarce rants at all:
He's somewhat lewd; but a well-meaning mind;
Weeps much; fights little; but is wond'rous kind.
In short, a Pattern, and Companion fit,
For all the keeping Tonyes of the Pit.
I cou'd name more: A Wife, and Mistress too;
Both (to be plain) too good for most of you:
The Wife well-natur'd, and the Mistress true.

Despite the evident banter and exaggeration of these lines, Dryden seems to be informing his audience that they should expect not only new versification but new conceptions of character. The play itself bears out his warning. Octavia is introduced as the symbol of the family. Although she speaks in the name of the Roman empire, her role in the play is really defined by her domestic relationships: as a wife, as a mother, and as a sister. Like Melisinda she is an abused wife, and like her also she is loyal and "well-natur'd"; she leaves Antony only after she has exacted from him, from Ventidius, from Dollabella, and from the audience, a full measure of the thrills of domestic piety. Her reconciliation scene with Antony is a paradigm of sentimental drama. She enters, *"leading* Antony's *two little Daughters,"* and she and Antony stage a brief debate in what appears to be the old style, "a strife of sullen Honour." But she confesses her love, Antony has to stifle a tear, and as Antony himself makes clear, the debate shifts from honor to pity. "Pity," he says, "pleads for *Octavia*; / But does it not plead more for Cleopatra?" Ventidius answers that "Justice and Pity both plead for *Octavia*," and Antony admits to a "distracted Soul."

[129]

The maudlin resolution of the scene is worth quoting
at length:

> *Octav.* Sweet Heav'n, compose it.
> Come, come, my Lord, if I can pardon you,
> Methinks you should accept it. Look on these;
> Are they not yours? Or stand they thus neglected
> As they are mine? Go to him, Children, go;
> Kneel to him, take him by the hand, speak to him,
> For you may speak, and he may own you too,
> Without a blush; and so he cannot all
> His Children: go, I say, and pull him to me,
> And pull him to yourselves from that bad Woman.
> You, *Agrippina*, hang upon his arms;
> And you, *Antonia*, clasp about his waste:
> If he will shake you off, if he will dash you
> Against the Pavement, you must bear it, Children;
> For you are mine, and I was born to suffer.
>> [*Here the Children go to him, &c.*
> *Ven.* Was ever sight so moving! Emperor!
> *Dolla.* Friend!
> *Octav.* Husband!
> *Both Childr.* Father!
> *Ant.* I am vanquish'd: take me,
> *Octavia*; take me, Children; share me all.
>> (*Embracing them*)
> I've been a thriftless Debtor to your loves,
> And run out much, in riot, from your stock;
> But all shall be amended.
> *Octav.*   O blest hour!
> *Dolla.* O happy change!
> *Ven.*   My joy stops at my tongue,
> But it has found two chanels here for one,
> And bubbles out above.
> *Ant. to Octav.* This is thy Triumph; lead me
>   where thou wilt;

Ev'n to thy Brother's Camp.
> *Octav.*   All there are yours.

(pp. 37, 39, 40-41; V, 389-91)

Dryden may have had reason to regret the division of pity which such a scene caused, but its tears and sentiment are not inconsistent with the affective emphasis in the rest of the play. Cleopatra, though somewhat less masochistic than Octavia, is similarly domesticated and sentimentally self-indulgent. In one speech she complains that "Nature meant" her to be "A Wife, a silly harmless household Dove, / Fond without art; and kind without deceit" (p. 47; V, 399), and although these lines can be misleading out of context, they do nonetheless describe her wishes accurately. In spirit, if not in name, she is indeed a suffering wife: utterly "true," as Dryden describes her in the prologue, utterly without the sexual independence which characterizes the heroines of Dryden's earlier plays. "She dotes, / She dotes . . . on this vanquish'd Man" (p. 3; V, 346), Alexas remarks, and she herself bewails "the curse / Of doting on, ev'n when I find it Dotage!" (p. 63; V, 418) Although she proclaims the heroism of this dotage and its simplicity (her love, she insists, is "plain, direct and open"), the play's emphasis is not upon the magnanimity of her fidelity but upon the hardships which she must endure because of it. Her major scenes are those in which she must face the loss of Antony, and in all them she proves herself by the sincerity of her grief. When Dollabella pretends that Antony has cast her off unkindly, "*she sinks quite down*" on the stage (p. 50; V, 402), and after her encounter with Octavia, she exits to a "solitary Chamber,"

> . . . to take alone
> My fill of grief:
> There I till death will his unkindness weep

[131]

As harmless Infants moan themselves asleep.
(p. 44; V, 395)

Cleopatra is heroic, worthy of Antony, not because she is a queen and a woman infinite in variety, but because she suffers and deserves pity, as she herself is quick to point out to Octavia:

> Yet she who loves him best is *Cleopatra*.
> If you have suffer'd, I have suffer'd more.
> You bear the specious Title of a Wife,
> To guild your Cause, and draw the pitying World
> To favour it: the World contemns poor me;
> For I have lost my Honour, lost my Fame,
> And stain'd the glory of my Royal House,
> And all to bear the branded Name of Mistress.
> There wants but life, and that too I would lose
> For him I love.
(p. 44; V, 394)

Antony, too, is willing to sacrifice all for love, and in him the accent on suffering and compassion is even more marked. Not "altogether wicked, because he could not then be pitied," he is as different from the heroical hero of Dryden's earlier plays as he is from Shakespeare's hero. Indecisive, and the constant prey of conflicting sentiments, he is thrown by the successive pleas of Ventidius, Octavia, Dollabella, and Cleopatra into alternating postures of grief and hope; and his ability to assume such postures with extravagance and tears becomes the final measure of his heroism. Early in the play Ventidius accords Antony the credentials of the earlier heroes: a "vast soul" and Herculean divinity:

> Methinks you breath
> Another Soul: Your looks are more Divine;
> You speak a Heroe, and you move a God.
(pp. 5, 14; V, 347, 359)

[132]

But the context of Ventidius' praise is a scene which exploits precisely those qualities in Antony which make him less than a god: his compassionate sensibilities, and his "tender heart." Antony gives in to Ventidius in this scene and agrees to resume the duties of his empire less to assert his glory than to demonstrate his affection for his friend. He hugs Ventidius and weeps with him:

> Sure there's contagion in the tears of Friends:
> See, I have caught it, too. Believe me, 'tis not
> For my own griefs, but thine.
>
> (p. 9; V, 353)

His relationship with Cleopatra, though more complicated, is similarly sentimental; heroic issues again are essentially excuses for the exercise of emotion. Antony claims often that Cleopatra "deserves / More World's than I can lose" (p. 12; V, 357), but when the play begins he has already effectively lost the world and we see him *"walking with a disturb'd Motion,"* and shortly afterwards, lying prostrate upon the stage. Antony proves his worth as a lover much as Cleopatra does, not by giving away worlds which are no longer in his power to give, but by showing his capacity for sympathy and suffering. He can almost always be reduced to tears by his friends and by her—"One look of hers, would thaw me into tears," he tells Dollabella, "And I should melt until I were lost agen." (p. 45; V, 395)—and in virtually every situation in which we see him on stage, his grandeur is shown by the enormity of his distress. No longer a conqueror, a family man rather than a superman, Antony is the hero of a play which exalts the man of feeling, the man who *"Weeps much; fights little; but is wond'rous kind."*[7]

---

[7] The weeping of the men in *All for Love* is especially conspicuous. Antony cries three times onstage (pp. 9, 39, 62-63; V, 353,

The sentimentalization of character and action in *All for Love* can be explained, in part, as the extension of experiments and tendencies in Dryden's earlier plays. Isolated characters such as Acacis in *The Indian Queen* and Ozmyn and Benzayda in *The Conquest of Granada* are conspicuously pathetic, and *Aureng-Zebe,* as we have seen, is sentimental both in structure and characterization. But the change in style in *All for Love,* as well as in *Aureng-Zebe* itself, is also the consequence of developments in the drama of Dryden's contemporaries, particularly in the plays of Nathaniel Lee and Thomas Otway. Both Lee and Otway were innovators and although in certain respects they were quite different, together they helped create a new sentimental style on the English stage in the late 1670's. They were both exceptionally popular dramatists, and a good number of their plays had been performed before Dryden began writing *All for Love* in the spring of 1677, including four of Lee's tragedies: *Nero, Sophonisba, Gloriana,* and *The Rival Queens;* and three of Otway's: *Alcibiades, Don Carlos,* and *Titus and Berenice.*[8]

Otway wrote for the rival Duke's Company. Dryden appears to have been aware of his early success and may have been provoked by him to exploit sentimental effects

---

388, 417) and once his "falling tear" is reported. (p. 17; V, 362) Dollabella cries when Antony exiles him (pp. 62-63; V, 417) and even Ventidius cries twice, once in grief for Antony (p. 9; V, 352) and once in joy over Antony's family reunion. (p. 41; V, 390)

[8] Lee made his debut with *The Tragedy of Nero* in May 1674 (published 1675), followed by *Sophonisba* in April 1675 (published 1676), *Gloriana* in January 1675/76 (published 1676), and *The Rival Queens* in March 1676/77 (published 1677). The first play of Otway to be performed was *Alcibiades,* in September 1675 (published 1675), followed by *Don Carlos* in June 1676 (published 1676) and *Titus and Berenice* c. December 1676 (published 1677). Otway also wrote two comedies during this period, *The Cheats of Scapin* and *Friendship in Fashion.*

in his own plays.[9] *Alcibiades* preceded *Aureng-Zebe* by approximately two months on the stage, and although no specific influence can be demonstrated with certainty, the plays are similar. Like *Aureng-Zebe*, *Alcibiades* is a mélange of heroism and sentiment, exalting "distrest lovers," repudiating libertinism, and emphasizing the heroic qualities of family piety, forgiveness and, of course, tears.[10] There are at least two scenes in Otway's play, moreover, that may have been especially suggestive

[9] The personal relations between Dryden and Otway are not clear, but Otway seems to imply in his preface to *Don Carlos* that Dryden was jealous of his success. See Macdonald, *John Dryden*, p. 212.

[10] The central heroic pair of the play are Alcibiades and Timandra, whose love and worth are virtually defined by their capacity for unending distress and frustration. Timandra, for example, tests Alcibiades by observing the measure of his grief when he has been given a false report of her death, and she imagines their ultimate marriage as the occasion for the recapitulation of their woes:

> And when our faithful happy hearts shall be
> Nearer united by that sacred tye,
> How in an endless Road of bliss we'l move,
> Steering our motions by our perfect Love!
> There we with pleasure will recount each woe
> Which we have pass't, and others undergoe.
> There we'll reflect o'th' various hopes and fears,
> The mournful sighs and the impatient tears
> Of distrest Lovers. . . .

(*The Works of Thomas Otway*, ed. J. C. Ghosh, 2 vols. [Oxford, 1932], I, 114). Both lovers are harassed throughout the play, and they die, unrequited, in a bath of sentiment and tears.

The play as a whole abounds in tears and familial sentiments (see especially the behavior and speeches of Draxilla and Patroclus, Ghosh, I, 110-11, 124, 126-27, 130) and libertinism is unequivocally condemned. Alcibiades, for example, is shocked by the blandishments of the lustful queen, Deidamia, and he spurns her with Platonic arguments:

> . . . only be as truly good,
> As you are fair, I shall not need be woo'd,
> I'le love you as the Sister of my blood.
>
> (Ghosh, I, 134)

to Dryden: one in which the heroine, Timandra, and her friend, Draxilla, sing a duet of mutual pity, and another in which Timandra forgives her libertine suitor on his deathbed.[11] In his succeeding tragedies, *Don Carlos* and *Titus and Berenice*, the latter a free translation of Racine, Otway concentrated even more exclusively upon pathos. Both plays deal with thwarted love and its attendant despair and distraction, and both were frankly designed, as Otway said in the preface to *Don Carlos*, "to draw Tears from the Eyes of the Auditors, I mean those whose Souls were capable of so Noble a pleasure." (Ghosh, I, 174) In addition, both plays, *Titus and Berenice* especially, deal explicitly with the theme which occupies Dryden in *All for Love*, the choice of love at the expense of empire and glory.[12] Otway's influence upon Dryden should certainly not be exaggerated. Dryden never tried, and was probably temperamentally unable to imitate Otway's characteristic pathetic fantasies. "The power that predominated in [Dryden's] intellectual operations," as Dr. Johnson noted,[13] "was rather strong reason than quick sensibility." But Otway may still have stimulated him to develop his own sentimental style in *Aureng-Zebe* and *All for Love* and unquestionably helped to provide a theatrical climate in which such a style could flourish.

Lee's relationship to Dryden is less conjectural. Both wrote for the same company and by 1677 they knew

---

[11] Cf. *Alcibiades* (Ghosh, I, 110-11, and 139); and *Aureng-Zebe* (sigs. F-Fv; V, 240-42, and pp. 68-69; V, 280-82).

[12] See, *e.g.*, *Titus and Berenice* (Ghosh, I, 273, 282, and 291). Examples simply of sentimental and tearful scenes in *Titus* and *Don Carlos* are too numerous to cite.

[13] *Lives of the English Poets*, ed. Hill, I, 457. It is significant that in his later plays Dryden concentrated upon scenes of sentiment between men: *e.g.*, Antony and Ventidius in *All for Love*, Hector and Troilus in *Troilus and Cressida*, Sebastian and Dorax in *Don Sebastian*, and Cleomenes and Cleanthes in *Cleomenes*. Otway usually placed great emphasis upon his female characters.

each other personally. In that year Lee wrote an epistle to *The State of Innocence* and Dryden replied with commendatory verses to *The Rival Queens*. In succeeding years they exchanged prologues, epilogues, and epistles, and collaborated on two plays: *Oedipus* (1679) and *The Duke of Guise* (1683). Contemporary writers seem to have taken a close professional relationship between the two men for granted, and it is safe to assume that Dryden both knew Lee's early plays and learned from them.[14]

Lee's most successful and influential plays were *Sophonisba* and *The Rival Queens*, but even *Nero* and *Gloriana* may have been suggestive to Dryden. *Nero*, Lee's first play, is frequently derivative: the whole conception of the play is indebted to Dryden's earlier tragedies and the lustful, ranting Nero is an obvious copy of Maximin. But the play also looks forward to Dryden's later plays. Nero, for example, is castigated for his libertine pride by Seneca in terms that are similar to those which Indamora uses to rebuke the ambition of Morat,[15] and as in *Aureng-Zebe* and *All for Love*, the ethical and dramatic focus of the play is upon sentiment. All of the major characters (including Nero) and most of the attendants weep during the play; pity is specifically invoked as a cardinal virtue on several occasions;[16] and Nero's acts of cruelty and libertinism are explored both for their own sakes and as a means of generating scenes of pathos and distress. *Gloriana*, Lee's third play, has a similar sentimental bias. As in *Nero*, scenes of weeping are frequent (Narcissa, aptly named, dies of

[14] For a discussion of Dryden's relations with Lee, see Roswell G. Ham, *Otway and Lee* (New Haven, 1931), pp. 156-57, 235-36, notes 1 and 2.

[15] Cf. *Nero* (*The Works of Nathaniel Lee*, eds. T. B. Stroup and A. L. Cooke, 2 vols. [New Brunswick, 1954], I, 32-33) and *Aureng-Zebe* (pp. 68-69; V, 280-82).

[16] See, *e.g.*, Stroup and Cooke, I, 28, 55, 61, 68.

grief), and the court of Augustus is thoroughly domesticated. Augustus himself concludes the play with the
comment:

> So Heav'n abroad with Conquest crowns my Wars,
> But wracks my spirit with domestick jars.
> (Stroup and Cooke, I, 207)

It is, however, in *Sophonisba* and *The Rival Queens*
that the more specific and important anticipations of Dryden are to be found. *Sophonisba*, Lee's first unqualified
stage success, foreshadows *All for Love* in its treatment
both of love and of friendship. There are two romantic
intrigues in the play, one dealing with the love of
Hannibal and Rosalinda, the other with the love of
Massinissa and Sophonisba. Both are predicated on the
supposition that love is worth more than glory, and both
accentuate the pathetic and ultimately tragic predica-
ments of the lovers. Hannibal, whom the Earl of
Rochester stigmatized as "a whining, Amorous slave,"[17]
announces near the opening of the play that

> Melting at Capua I in pleasures lay,
> And for a Mistriss gave the World away.
> (Stroup and Cooke, I, 87)

In the course of the action he loses his empire and his
mistress, who is killed in battle disguised as a boy. The
situation of Massinissa is even closer to Antony's because, like Dryden's hero, he is torn not simply by
verbal debate between the values of empire and the
values of love, but by a concrete dramatic conflict between the claims of his friend and the claims of his mistress. Scipio, Massinissa's ruler and friend, a prototype
of Ventidius, urges him to be true to their friendship
and to their common Roman ideals, while Sophonisba
appeals to him to protect her from the Romans and to
be true to love. Affected almost equally by both claims,

[17] Cited in Stroup and Cooke, I, 76.

Massinissa for most of the play is depicted precisely like Antony, in alternating pathetic postures of friendship or love.[18] Like Antony also, he eventually remains true to his mistress. Towards the end of the play he marries Sophonisba, and when Scipio refuses to allow him to keep her, they commit suicide together. Massinissa tells her as they are dying: "Thy love is Empire and eternal bliss." (Stroup and Cooke, I, 142)

Lee habitually adapted lines, characters, and situations from Shakespeare and there are enough echoes of *Antony and Cleopatra* in *Sophonisba* to indicate that Shakespeare's play was the model for the conception of Massinissa and Sophonisba. Dryden, in writing his own adaptation of *Antony and Cleopatra*, is therefore likely to have been susceptible to Lee's earlier and very popular experiment.

The Rival Queens, Lee's next important play, was an even greater hit than *Sophonisba*, and it was performed in March 1677, precisely the time Dryden was writing *All for Love*.[19] Its unusual success would have made an impression on any contemporary dramatist. "There was no one tragedy, for many years," Colley Cibber remarked, "more in favour with the town than ALEXANDER,"[20] and Cibber himself was able to write a popular parody of it in 1710, thirty-three years after its initial performance.

The Rival Queens is a culmination of the themes and characters of Lee's earlier plays, especially *Sophonisba*. Its hero, Alexander, like Hannibal and Massinissa, willingly disposes "of Crowns and Scepters"[21] for the sake

---

[18] For examples of Massinissa's conflict between love and glory, see Stroup and Cooke, I, 88-91, 95-98, 113-18, 130, 140.

[19] See Charles E. Ward, *The Life of John Dryden* (Chapel Hill, 1961), pp. 119-20.

[20] Cited in Stroup and Cooke, I, 213.

[21] Stroup and Cooke, I, 254. For other examples of the theme of all for love in the play, see *ibid.*, pp. 228, 247, 257, 259.

of his love. As with Massinissa also, his passionate lapse from glory is steadily opposed by a blunt, stoic, and devoted soldier, Clytus, the counterpart of Scipio and several other soldierly advisers in *Sophonisba*. Alexander's principal distinction from his predecessors is that he has two lovers rather than one, the rival queens of the title: Statira, his virtuous and jealous wife, and Roxana, the raging and jealous mistress whom he has abandoned. The action of the play, however, is basically similar to that of *Sophonisba*: a series of peripatetic situations which elicit from Alexander a variety of extravagant displays of emotion as he alternately confronts his mistress, his wife, and his friend. He dies, like Massinissa, true to the glory "In his heart."

Dryden clearly had Lee's play specifically in mind as he wrote *All for Love*. To begin with, the conception of an active rivalry between Cleopatra and Octavia, including a confrontation between the two characters on stage, is undoubtedly indebted to the popularity of Lee's rival ladies. There was absolutely no warrant for such a scene in Shakespeare, and there was in Lee. Dryden's reservations in the dedication to the play about his introduction of Octavia is, in fact, a tacit admission that in this matter he was following a theatrical fashion. Dryden's debt to Lee is also evident in his characterization of the relationship between Ventidius and Antony, and this debt is significant because Dryden was especially proud of his portrait of the friendship between the two men. He wrote in the dedication to *All for Love*: "I prefer the scene betwixt Anthony and Ventidius in the first Act to any thing which I have written in this kind." The suggestion for this scene almost certainly came from Lee: Ventidius is virtually a carbon copy of Clytus and the sentimental attachment between him and Antony duplicates exactly the relationship between Clytus and

Alexander, as well as between Scipio and Massinissa.[22] Moreover, Dryden wrote the parts of Antony and Ventidius for Hart and Mohun, the same actors who nine months earlier had played the roles of Alexander and Clytus. Hart, in addition, had created the role of Massinissa.

There seems little question, therefore, that in his later tragedies, Dryden was responding to the new directions that were being charted by his young and successful contemporaries. *Aureng-Zebe* and particularly *All for Love* must be understood not simply as an extension of his earlier rhymed tragedies, but as his response to the new developments in the theater of the late 1670's. Dryden was a competitor of Otway and a close associate of Lee. He probably owed, as we have seen, specific debts to both dramatists, to Lee especially, and he was certainly influenced by their general, and revolutionary anticipations of sentimental drama. In his epistle to *The Rival Queens*, Dryden praised the "Fire" with which Lee animated his themes, the beauty of his "Images," and above all else, his mastery in painting the passions:

> Such praise is yours, while you the Passions move,
> That 'tis no longer feign'd; 'tis real Love,
> Where Nature Triumphs over wretched Art;
> We only warm the Head, but you the Heart.
>
> (Stroup and Cooke, I, 222)

The terms of Dryden's praise are conventional, but the distinctions he makes are significant because the conventional terms now had new meanings. Dryden had always acknowledged the passions to be the dramatist's peculiar province—*Of Dramatick Poesie* was written on that assumption—but the passions now, as Lee and Otway helped show him, were differently conceived

[22] Cf., *e.g.*, *Sophonisba* (II, i), *The Rival Queens* (IV, ii) and *All for Love* (I, i).

and demanded a different dramatic orientation in depicting them.

(iii) *Troilus and Cressida*

Both *Troilus and Cressida* and its preface confirm
Dryden's commitment to this new orientation. The play
itself is less consistently pathetic than *All for Love*, but
its sentimentalism is still unmistakable. Cressida, like
Cleopatra is made transparently faithful; and Troilus,
like Antony, is portrayed in a series of tableaux of grief
and hope; Hector, the play's most exemplary character,
numbers as a principal heroic virtue his devotion as a
husband and a brother. All three characters, but especially the men, are distinguished by their ability to feel
compassion for one another. Hector is valiant, but
Andromache's highest praise of him is that his "Soul
is proof to all things but to kindness." (p. 59; VI, 374)
Troilus, younger and more demonstrative than Hector,
shows his mettle by tears and distraction. During their
farewell scene he and Cressida *"both weep over each
other"* (p. 41; VI, 348), and after Cressida kills herself
to prove her fidelity to him, he demonstrates his own
love by the extremity of his grief:

> . . . she dy'd for me;
> And like a woman, I lament for her:
> Distraction pulls me several ways at once,
> Here pity calls me to weep out my eyes;
> Despair then turns me back upon my self,
> And bids me seek no more, but finish here:
> > [*Sword to his breast.*
> > (p. 68; VI, 388)

The play's most celebrated scene, added by Dryden at
the suggestion of Betterton, shows Troilus and Hector
debating whether to surrender Cressida to the Greeks.
The dispute has the same turns and counterturns as the

rhymed debates in Dryden's earlier plays, but the crux of the argument is now plainly the point of pity rather than the point of honor. After Troilus agrees to give Cressida up, Hector tells him, "I pity thee, indeed I pity thee," and Troilus answers:

> Do; for I need it: let me lean my head
> Upon thy bosome; all my peace dwells there;
> Thou art some God, or much much more than man!

In a final turn, Hector offers to fight to keep Cressida in Troy, but Troilus refuses: "That you have pitied me is my reward"; and Hector concedes: "The triumph of this kindeness be thy own." (p. 40; VI, 346-47)

The triumph of kindness is evident in the preface to the play as well. Dryden discusses tragedy primarily in affective terms, and although he parrots Rapin and Rymer in paying homage to both sides of the Aristotelian formula, his emphasis is clearly upon pity. *"When we see,"* he writes, *"that the most virtuous, as well as the greatest, are not exempt from . . . misfortunes, that consideration moves pity in us: and insensibly works us to be helpfull to, and tender over the distress'd, which is the noblest and most God-like of moral virtues."* (sig. a2v; VI, 263) Dryden praises both Shakespeare and Beaumont and Fletcher for their ability to stimulate this virtue. He praises *"the lively touches of the passions"* in Beaumont and Fletcher's plays and remarks that *A King and no King* is the *"best of their designs, the most approaching to Antiquity, and the most conducing to move pity."* (sig. [a3]; VI, 264) He commends Shakespeare especially for *"passionate descriptions,"* and cites as an example the depiction of Richard II after his deposition: *"Suppose you have seen already the fortunate Usurper passing through the croud, and follow'd by the shouts and acclamations of the people; and now behold King Richard entring upon the Scene: consider the wretchedness of his condition, and his carriage in it; and refrain from pitty if you can."* (sig. [b3]; VI, 281)

This critical emphasis upon pity, upon the audience's "concernment" for the "sufferings" of the hero, compels Dryden to reconsider his earlier theory of tragedy. He now, for example, categorically condemns the villain as hero: " . . . *it is absolutely necessary to make a man virtuous, if we desire he should be pity'd: We lament not, but detest a wicked man, we are glad when we behold his crimes are punish'd, and that Poetical justice is done upon him. . . ."* (sig. a2v; VI, 263) On the same premise, Dryden unequivocally repudiates the style of his earlier rhymed plays. He speaks first of the danger of writing in a style that is sustained at a consistently high pitch, a pitch that he had formerly both practiced and justified: *". . . the Passions, as they are consider'd simply and in themselves, suffer violence when they are perpetually maintain'd at the same height; for what melody can be made on that Instrument all whose strings are screw'd up at first to their utmost stretch, and to the same sound? But this is not the worst; for the Characters likewise bear a part in the general calamity, if you consider the Passions as embody'd in them: for it follows of necessity, that no man can be distinguish'd from another by his discourse, when every man is ranting, swaggering, and exclaiming with the same excess."* (sig. bv; VI, 276) In discussing how passion is to be raised in an audience, Dryden subjects his earlier practice to even harsher criticism: *"There is yet another obstacle to be remov'd* [for the proper *"moving of the passions"*], *which is pointed Wit, and Sentences affected out of season; these are nothing of kin to the violence of passion: no man is at leisure to make sentences and similes, when his soul is in an Agony. I the rather name this fault, that it may serve to mind me of my former*

[144]

errors; neither will I spare my self, but give an example of this kind from my Indian Emperour. Montezuma, *pursu'd by his enemies, and seeking Sanctuary, stands parlying without the Fort, and describing his danger to* Cydaria, *in a simile of six lines;*

> As on the sands the frighted Traveller
> Sees the high Seas come rowling from afar, *&c.*

My Indian Potentate was well skill'd in the Sea for an Inland Prince, and well improv'd since the first Act, when he sent his son to discover it. The Image had not been amiss from another man, at another time: Sed nunc non erat hisce locus: *he destroy'd the concernment which the Audience might otherwise have had for him; for they could not think the danger near, when he had the leisure to invent a Simile.*" (sig. b2; VI, 278)

The basis of this argument is the principle of decorum, the same principle by which, a decade earlier, Dryden had defended the use of rhyme and figurative expression, but he applied it now, as he had never before done, to the verisimilitude of the subject represented.[23] "*Nothing of kin*" is a phrase which Howard would have embraced in the heyday of their quarrel over rhyme. In using it, Dryden repudiated the assumption that had supported his rhymed plays and declared his allegiance to the sentimental drama of his younger contemporaries. Two years later, in the dedication of *The Spanish Fryar,* he recanted his earlier style completely: "*I remember some Verses of my own* Maximin *and* Almanzor *which cry, Vengeance upon me for their Extravagance . . . All I can say for those passages, which are I hope not many, is, that I knew they were bad enough to please, even when I writ them: But I repent of them amongst my*

---

[23] For a detailed discussion of the critical background of Dryden's change, see Eric Rothstein, "English Tragic Theory in the Late Seventeenth Century," *ELH,* XXIX (1962), 306-23.

Sins: *and if any of their fellows intrude by chance into my present Writings, I draw a stroke over all those* Dalilahs *of the Theatre. . . . Neither do I discommend the lofty style in Tragedy which is naturally pompous and magnificent: but nothing is truly sublime that is not just and proper.*" (sigs. A2v-A3; VI, 406-07)

CHAPTER V

Conclusion

DRYDEN wrote in the prologue to *Aureng-Zebe* that he was

> . . . betwixt two ages cast
> The first of this, and hindmost of the last.

The remark is true of his dramatic temperament as well as of his historical position, and it offers us perhaps the single most important insight into the nature and development of his heroic drama. Both individually and as a group, his heroic plays must be understood in the context of, and as a product of, a theater which was poised between two dramatic traditions.

Despite his own enthusiasm about his epic innovations and the novelty of his dramatic verse, most of the salient features of Dryden's early plays are derived from the Jacobean and Caroline court stage. There is no need to rehearse these features in detail: complicated plots, characters and action responding to the laws of spatial design rather than to the demands of logic or psychology, a disposition for fine writing, including stylized verse, elaborate figurative descriptions, and a proliferation of witty debates—all of these characteristics dominate Dryden's plays from *The Rival Ladies* to *The Conquest of Granada* and all of them are typical of the earlier tradition of Fletcherian tragicomedy. Dryden's relationship to this tradition, moreover, goes even deeper than these specific debts suggest, for, as we have seen, he inherited from Jacobean and Caroline court drama the very idea of theater upon which his earlier heroic plays are based. The defining characteristic of this theater was a calculated balance between artifice and illusion, between detachment and engagement. To refer

[147]

once again to James Shirley's description of the form: *"You may here find passions raised to that excellent pitch and by such insinuating degrees that you shall not chuse but consent, & go along with them, finding yourself at last grown insensibly the very same person you read, and then stand admiring the subtile trackes of your engagement."* Dryden's rhymed plays not only conform to this conception of drama but are almost conscious attempts to keep it viable.

Sentiment and sentimental effects began to encroach upon serious drama even in the early years of the Restoration. The Fletcherian pattern from the first had strong affective elements—the pathos of Aspatia is unsurpassable—and had demanded considerable subtlety in maintaining the requisite balance between passion and artifice. With less skill and under increasing pressure for novelty, Fletcher's successors had preserved this poise only by grossly exaggerating both the sentiments and the style. Late Caroline court drama, for example, is guilty simultaneously of hyperbolic style and sensational and often sentimental characters and situations; and by the time of the Restoration this rather precarious balance had nearly dissolved. Roger Boyle is a case in point. The verse and structure of his plays are rigidly geometric and stylized, encouraging a detached observation of their own contrivance; and yet both the verse and the structure are repeatedly threatened by doses of sentiment. The unrequited lover, for example, appears in every one of Boyle's plays, frequently dominating them, and the *précieux* behavior of even the successful lovers almost always impinges upon the wit and geometry of their encounters.

Dryden's rhymed plays do not suffer from this imbalance. At least for a while, he managed to stem the tide of sentiment and to perpetuate the Fletcherian tradition. As we have seen, there are unmistakable sentimental elements even in his early plays. Like Boyle, Dryden has his share of unrequited and sentimental lovers—Acacis, for example, who dies refreshed by "a kind shower of pittying tears," and Ozmyn and Benzayda, who luxuriate in domestic sentiment and self-sacrifice. But unlike Boyle, Dryden, in his earlier plays, keeps these sentimental elements in a minor key. They are usually used as contrasts to heighten the grandeur of the heroic characters, and even when they are exploited for their own sake, they are integrated into the total structure of the play. Montezuma neutralizes Acacis' sentimentalism as Almanzor more than compensates for the pathetic trials of Ozmyn and Benzayda; and there is no question in either play as to who is the hero. Thus we can be affected by Dryden's appeals to pity in these plays at the same time that the structure as a whole permits us to be conscious of his craft in making the appeal. This is essentially the Fletcherian pattern, very similar to the manner in which Aspatia is handled in *The Maid's Tragedy*.

Dryden kept this pattern alive on the English stage primarily because he was able to vary it without violating it. The use of rhymed verse and the exploitation of the super-hero—both of which he rightly regarded as his distinctive contributions to English drama—are also, paradoxically, essentially traditional. In both cases, as we have seen, Dryden may have been helped by "*the example* of Corneille," but his debts to Corneille do not contradict his English heritage. Corneille's plays are cast in the same pattern as Fletcher's and they depend upon the same Continental tradition of tragicomedy to which Fletcher himself was indebted. The really radical conception of tragedy in France came with the drama of Racine; Corneille's, like Dryden's, was essentially traditional. Corneille had exploited the heroic and verbal possibilities of tragicomedy with outstanding success: he was popular not only with the French but with the English aristocracy that constituted Dryden's early audience. It was thus almost inevitable both that Dryden should have followed Corneille's precedents and that these precedents should have been entirely compatible with the native English tradition. The heroic couplet is no different in kind from the declamatory verse of Fletcher and his successors: both are consciously rhetorical, designed at once to move an audience and to reveal the art which moves them. Dryden exploited the couplet because it was congenial to him and because he saw the chance of doing with it what no one in England had done before, but its dramatic effect was not revolutionary. Similarly, Dryden's super-heroes, though they owe much to the Cornélian concept of *gloire,* are also comprehensible as logical projections of characters like Fletcher's Arbaces. The kind of response which Arbaces demands from an audience is a mixture of concernment and detachment: we are moved by the course of his passion and yet his discontinuous characterization, his Protean changes, compel us to stand back and admire the tracks of our engagement. The same is true of our response to Almanzor or Montezuma or Maximin: all the devices of the theater encourage us to believe in them and even to sympathize with them; yet their very extravagance, especially their verbal extravagance, forces us to admire them as patent demonstrations of dramatic wit.

Dryden's rhymed plays, therefore, maintain the balance between engagement and detachment which had characterized English aristocratic drama from the early seventeenth century, but they also reveal the cost at which he kept his allegiance to this tradition. Compared to Fletcherian drama, the rhymed heroic plays are frequently limited and strained; and compared to Cornélian drama, they are unnatural.[1] Dryden was a master of the couplet, but at its best rhymed verse is not as natural or versatile a dramatic medium as blank verse; and there are many scenes in Dryden's plays in which the verse is flaccid and tedious. The designs of his plays, though not as geometrically repetitive as Boyle's, are nevertheless quite restricted, and his heroical heroes tread a perilous line between magnificence and self-parody. By the time he wrote *Aureng-Zebe* these intrinsic difficulties had begun to alter the direction of his drama.[2]

This change of direction, however, was not simply nor primarily a matter of personal exhaustion. The movement of English taste seems to have made it inevitable. There was a comparable change in Restoration comedy, with the admirable and libertine rake-hero giving way to the exemplary and moral man of feeling. As we have seen, the heroes of Dryden's plays and of early Restoration comedies have much in common. Al-

[1] In a sense, what Dryden was doing in the heroic play was exploring the operatic possibilities latent within the Fletcherian pattern. He would have been encouraged in this course by Davenant, whose *Siege of Rhodes* was first presented in recitative, and by the increasing emphasis during the Restoration upon movable scenery and stage effects which had previously been used only for masques. He would also have been encouraged by Corneille, for as W. H. Auden has observed, French classical theater is essentially operatic in its conception and delivery of dramatic verse. The difficulty, however, as Auden has also noted, is that whereas opera has flourished in France, it has always been alien to the English tradition; and the difference in quality between Dryden's plays and Corneille's can be traced, at least in part, to this fact. After Dryden there was no serious effort in England to exploit the operatic resources of drama until the plays of Shaw.

[2] Frank Harper Moore, *The Nobler Pleasure* (Chapel Hill, 1963), pp. 126-66, notes a significant change in Dryden's comedies at the same time as I have argued his tragedy changed. Moore interprets the shift in terms that are different from mine, but his analysis confirms a fundamental change in Dryden's dramatic practice during the mid and late 1670's.

manzor's actions are complicated by aspirations to super-
virtues to which the untroubled libertinism of such a
figure as Dorimant rarely pretends, and the pitch and
scope of their respective actions differ according to the
respective decorums of tragedy and comedy. But as contemporary reactions to the rhymed heroic play make
clear, both characters are actuated by a naturalistic ethic
of conquest. Both also flourish in a medium of accen-
tuated verbal wit. Towards the close of the Restoration
the wit and the libertinism faded in comedy and tragedy
and both the super-hero and the rake-hero gave way
to sentimental and domesticated protagonists.

One manifestation of the change, in tragedy, was the
increasing popularity of the "new" dramatists, Lee
and Otway; another was the attack upon the native
dramatic tradition which Rymer launched in *The
Tragedies of the Last Age* (1677). Rymer attacked all
the drama of what Dryden called the great age before
the flood, but he trained his sights particularly upon the
plays and dramatic assumptions of Beaumont and
Fletcher. In analyzing *The Maid's Tragedy*, for example, Rymer condemned the debate between Amintor
and Melantius over Evadne. Arguing on the premise
that the action must be literally credible if the audience
is to identify with it, Rymer criticized the witty turns
of the debate and mocked the frequency with which
Amintor and Melantius alternately brandish and put
up their swords. "*Harlequin* and *Scaramouttio* might do
these things," Rymer observes, "Tragedy suffers 'em
not, here is no place for Cowards, nor for giddy fellows,
and Bullies with their squabbles. When a Sword is once
drawn in Tragedy, the Scabbard may be thrown away;
there is no leaving what is once design'd, till it be
thoroughly effected. *Iphigenia Taurica* went to sacrifice
Orestes, and she desisted, why? she discover'd him to
be her Brother. None here are such Fools as by words

to begin a quarrel; nor of so little resolution, to be talkt agen from it, without some new emergent cause that diverts them. No simple alteration of mind ought to produce or hinder any action in a Tragedy."[3]

Such criticism is fatal to a drama which values its own artifice, and it is significant that revivals of Beaumont and Fletcher declined radically at this time. Rymer uses the traditional principles of decorum but he shifts the focus from the imitation itself to the thing imitated. In his later theory and practice, as we have seen, Dryden did the same. He repudiated the "Dalilahs" of his youth and, in *Aureng-Zebe* and the plays which followed it, abandoned the premises of his earlier drama. The balance between engagement and detachment gave way increasingly to an emphasis upon engagement alone. The admirable superman was replaced by a sympathetic *homme de famille,* the turns and counterturns of the action were muted and made more credible, and the versification became less stylized and less obtrusive. In his later criticism Dryden placed great stress upon his renewed respect for the drama before the Interregnum, particularly Shakespeare's, and like many of his contemporaries he began to write adaptations of Shakespeare's plays. But it would be most misleading to see his use of Shakespeare as a return to the earlier tradition. It was not. Dryden was much closer to this tradition when he claimed to be competing with it than when he professed to be following it. Shakespeare is infinitely adaptable and Dryden, as many dramatists since, exploited him for his own purposes. Dryden's later plays are conceived and executed on the principles of sentimental drama, and they represent a decisive break with the past. *All for Love* and *Troilus and*

[3] *The Critical Works of Thomas Rymer,* ed. Curt Zimansky (New Haven, 1956), p. 73. See above, Chapter III, section i, for a discussion of this scene.

Cressida, like *Aureng-Zebe,* are the harbingers of the prose drama of illusion and sentiment that is the heritage of the modern theater.

The most significant fact about Dryden's heroic drama, then, is that it changed with the theater for which it was written. Neither his theory nor his practice was static. Writing for a stage and society that were in transition, he was able both to capitalize upon the old and to explore the new. He was, as he himself realized, at once the last of the Elizabethans and the first of the Moderns, and if this position defines the limitations of his plays, it also contributes to their enduring interest and vitality.

INDEX

INDEX